THE LIST

THE LIST

SHOUT YOUR DREAMS OUT LOUD TO MAKE THEM COME TRUE

YUVAL ABRAMOVITZ

Skyhorse Publishing

Skyhorse Publishing books may be purchased in bulk at special discounts for sales promotion, corporate gifts, fund-raising, or educational purposes. Special editions can also be created to specifications. For details, contact the Special Sales Department, Skyhorse Publishing, 307 West 36th Street, 11th Floor, New York, NY 10018 or info@ skyhorsepublishing.com.

Skyhorse® and Skyhorse Publishing® are registered trademarks of Skyhorse Publishing, Inc.®, a Delaware corporation.

Visit our website at www.skyhorsepublishing.com.
10 9 8 7 6 5 4 3 2 1

Library of Congress Cataloging-in-Publication Data is available on file.

Cover design by Rain Saukas

Editor of the Hebrew edition: Anat Lev Adler

Print ISBN: 978-1-5107-1845-6
Ebook ISBN: 978-1-5107-1847-0

Printed in China

To my noble grandmother, the late Sophia Abramovitz, who had many dreams but was unable to realize them all.

To my beloved mother, Tamar Abramovitz, for raising me to always follow my heart.

And to my daughters, Shira and Noga, for helping me experience childhood for the second time around.

1 | THE LIST
THAT SAVED ME

AT THE TENDER AGE OF SIXTEEN, MY LIFE AS I KNEW IT AND THE LIFE I HAD IMAGINED FOR MYSELF WAS OVER. AN ACCIDENT HAD FLIPPED MY WORLD UPSIDE DOWN.

It all happened when I was working at a steakhouse as a busboy, clearing tables. The lowest in the food chain of hospitality jobs. I was saving money for all the things a boy my age would want—a driver's license, new clothes, and CDs.

During one shift I was asked to bring a heavy barrel of pickles from the storage located next to the restaurant.

In the parking lot, between the restaurant and the storage room, there was a small and extremely slippery puddle. It was a viscous trap of motor oil, cooking oil, and detergent residue that was washed out of the restaurant on a daily basis.

Two weeks prior to my accident, the owner of the restaurant had himself slipped on that puddle and broken his arm. Being a responsible boy, I had mentioned to him on several occasions that he should cover the slippery puddle with a wooden deck to prevent further accidents, but he chose to ignore my advice. Then, before two weeks could pass, it was my turn.

Flying through the air, I landed right on the sewage lid, pickles scattering all around me. To this day, I can still hear the cracking sound of my skull when it hit the cold concrete. I remember the feeling of my head being practically yanked off my neck and my brain shaking in my head from one side to the other like a ping-pong ball. The back of my now bleeding neck hurt so badly that I was completely oblivious to the devastating injury in my lower back.

Diners and restaurant workers gathered around me, checking to see if I was conscious.

I was lifted up by three men, while the owner, still wounded and in a cast, orchestrated the whole operation. People yelled out: "Get up! Let's see if you can walk!" But I could barely stand. I felt dizzy and vomited twice.

An ambulance arrived, and I was rushed to hospital where I was immediately sent for X-rays and other medical tests. I notified the doctor at the ER that I had no sensation in my legs whatsoever, but when the results came back showing no evidence of any spinal injury, I was sent home. The doctor's instructions were simple—lie in bed for three days on a warm electric blanket, and I'd be as good as new in no time. The pain would be gone.

And he was right. The pain *was* gone, but so was any sensation in my legs. I woke up on the third day and couldn't even get myself out of bed. I was completely paralyzed, unable to stand or walk. It was the strangest sensation, as if I were hallucinating. I kept saying to myself, "Get up! Stand on your feet now!" But I just couldn't do it.

I pinched my legs: nothing.

I scratched them with my fingernails: nothing. No sensation.

I found a pen on the floor nearby and pricked my flesh with it. The leg bled, but I couldn't feel any pain.

"Mom! I'm paralyzed... I can't move!" I screamed out. She rushed to my room and started yelling orders at me: "Try walking! Try standing!"

"It's probably just pins and needles," she said trying to remain calm, but I could see the panic in her eyes. She ran to the bathroom, grabbed a pair of tweezers, and started pinching my toes, my feet, my ankles, quickly working her way up my thighs.

I felt nothing.

My mother went and called a neighbor who was kind enough to carry me down to his car, and we drove to the nearest hospital. I was sent to the ER for an initial diagnosis. A solemn-faced doctor examined me with a reflex hammer and diagnosed a complete loss of sensation in the right leg and 60 percent function loss in the left one.

The suspected diagnosis: a spinal injury. Two hours later, I was sent to the neurological ward, where I was again hit with a reflex hammer and had electric currents run through my legs in the hope I would feel a tingle. The doctors were trying to determine just how far the paralysis had spread.

Three doctors, accompanied by an intrigued group of interns, came by my room to see with their own eyes what had become the ward's talk-of-the-day. They wanted to know if the paralysis had spread as far as my genitals. Luckily that area was unaffected, thanks for asking!

After an exhausting night of test after test, the doctors were frustrated. The X-rays showed no fracture of the spine. There was no explanation of the reason for my paralysis, or an estimate of when, or if, my legs would ever function again. What they did notice was a slight movement of the lower vertebrae.

After being hospitalized for almost two months, there was no change in my condition. When it seemed pointless to keep me there, I was rolled home in my wheelchair—my new set of limbs. It turned out the doctors had planned it so that my hospitalization period would become a sort of practice and preparation for my new life. The life of a crippled sixteen-year-old.

During my stay I could feel the doctors getting desperate, then losing hope in finding any cure for my condition. In a final effort to stimulate my nervous system, they transmitted electrical currents through my legs right up until the day of my discharge. Then, declaring defeat, they put me in a wheelchair and sent me home to my new life.

I did not return to the hospital, nor did I go back to school. I was an eleventh-grader whose only consolation was that, due to my new circumstances, I was exempt from doing homework or studying for exams.

My bedroom became the new social hub. From 8 a.m. till midnight my room was filled with school friends who came by to cheer me up. Sometimes I would have as many as twenty people at my bedside. I remember these days being so joyful and full of shared experiences: watching TV and movies together, gossiping about anyone and everyone, and my favorite activity of them all, making prank calls.

But after a while I'd had enough. The glamour of doing nothing and missing school expired, and I had to look reality in the eye. Despite my efforts to ignore the fact that I was paralyzed, life was providing me plenty of daily reminders. My close friends were going for their driver's licenses and planning their vacations. They were taking their final exams, falling in love, and their visits became more and more sporadic. I, on the other hand, was drawn more and more into a world of sickness, of physiotherapy sessions with geriatric patients who had broken their pelvises or suffered from heart diseases, patients who had lost their physical capacities and needed to relearn how to carry out simple tasks again. If that weren't enough, the cortisone shots I was given had completely deformed my body. This wasn't how I imagined my teenage years.

SOMETIMES PEOPLE ASK ME IF I WAS FEELING DEPRESSED DURING THAT TIME.
MY ANSWER IS SIMPLE: **I HAD NO TIME FOR IT. I WAS TOO BUSY PLANNING MY FUTURE.**

Out of boredom—but mainly because I wanted to get back on my feet so badly, and wholeheartedly believed that it would happen—I took an old school notebook and titled it *The List*. I began writing plans for the following year, at the end of which I would turn seventeen.

The page was filled with an endless list of goals, ambitions, and dreams. To start with, I began writing down ones that were directly related to my paralysis, but without noticing it I got carried further and further away in my imagination.

- ☐ Complete my final theatre exam
- ☐ Kiss for the first time
- ☐ Get a new computer
- ☐ Utilize my home stay to write a book
- ☐ Travel to London with my grandparents
- ☐ Perform in a musical by the time I'm twenty-five
- ☐ Climb the Great Wall of China by the age of thirty [preferably with my grandmother, who had dreamt about doing it her whole life]
- ☐ Work as a journalist and get my own personal column
- ☐ Act in a TV show, similar to the American sitcoms I watch on TV
- ☐ Establish an arts-related business

Having filled out two full pages of things I wanted to achieve by the age of seventeen, I turned a new leaf and started writing down a new list for my eighteenth year. Then for my nineteenth year, and so on, until I had reached the third and fourth decades of my life.

In less than a week I had a notebook full of plans, dreams, and goals to be accomplished and realized. Each time I had another idea for another goal, task or dream, I added it in the bottom of the relevant list. For example, on the "40 Years Old" page, I wrote, "Buy an apartment for cash." Even at my tender age I understood that mortgage is a risky business, so I had better start saving up!

In three years I will turn forty, and I'm still working hard to achieve that goal I set for myself twenty years ago.

One day a teacher came by for a visit. She saw the notebook with my scribbles all over and wondered what it was all about. I proudly shared my list idea and handed her the notebook.

She wanted to understand the motives behind each goal I wrote down. So I explained each and every one, but the more I let my imagination go, the sadder she became. I couldn't help but notice the moisture building up in her eyes and the expression on her face, as if saying, "Poor kid, not only is he physically paralyzed, he's now going insane too. He's completely lost any touch with reality."

I must admit, she wasn't the only one who felt that way toward me at the time. I got the same response from anyone who asked to read my notebook and found nothing in it but the unrealistic fantasies and pipe dreams of a young, disadvantaged boy.

Clearly, anyone in their right mind understands that you can't perform in a musical in a wheelchair (although *Glee* has since proven otherwise) or climb the Great Wall of China. Journalism is also a job that requires mobility and independence, and it was therefore deemed unrealistic. With the kind of medical restrictions I suffered, I clearly couldn't work, earn money, establish a business, or pay cash for an apartment (that one is hard enough standing firm on both feet, but that's another story). Deep down, though, I wanted to believe that one way or another I was going to realize all of these dreams.

Eventually, after twelve frustrating months of rehabilitation (including intensive and painful treatments) and long days of sitting in my wheelchair thinking and visualizing myself standing up again, and even giving interviews about my recovery story—I got on my feet and started walking.

It wasn't like in a Hollywood movie, where the war hero miraculously jumps out of his wheelchair and walks toward his one true love. It was a very long, exhausting, and difficult process. I had to endure many pitying stares from total strangers who saw my friends pushing me around in a wheelchair. Gradually, and agonizingly slowly, I moved from the wheelchair to a walker cushioned with tennis balls, then onto crutches, until I was finally able to stand on my own legs and walk those first shaky steps.

I will never forget that first day I was able to leave the house and visit a friend. It was the strangest feeling. I remember walking down my childhood streets, aiming my body forward, but somehow I was only moving diagonally. My brain needed to relearn how to direct my legs again.

I knocked on my friend's door, and when he opened it, we hugged, then went into his room as if it were a natural thing to do. It took him a minute before he realized I was actually standing on my own feet and he started screaming with excitement.

When my doctors heard I was walking again they had no explanation for it. Some of them tried to attribute it to a medical phenomenon called "drop foot," a kind of temporary paralysis caused by pressure inflicted by the vertebrae on the nervous system. Some doctors thought it a medical miracle, others believed it was the positive influence of oils and ointments that were massaged into my skin, or the religious charms and artifacts that were hung on my wheelchair.

One way or another, during those first days of spring, almost a year after the accident, I was back to a fully functioning life. Lacking a thoroughly convincing medical explanation for the cause of my recovery, I happily gave the same answer to anyone who asked me what happened.

✔ THE LIST I WROTE, **WITH ALL THE DREAMS I HAVE YET TO MATERIALIZE,** IS WHAT MOTIVATED ME TO GET BACK ON MY FEET AND WALK AGAIN. IT PRESENTED ME WITH GOALS AND FILLED ME **WITH HOPE** THAT **NOTHING** WOULD PREVENT ME FROM STANDING ON MY TWO FEET AND ACCOMPLISHING THEM.

MY LIST IS WHAT HELPED ME RISE UP FROM DESPAIR.

WHEN WE HAVE A DISTINCT GOAL WE ARE EAGER TO ACHIEVE, NO ROAD IS TOO LONG OR IMPOSSIBLE.

2 | THE BEST GIFT
I EVER RECEIVED

When I meet new people and share with them the story of my accident, I get the same reaction almost every time—shock and pity. They pity me for losing two of my best teenage years, and they are shocked at the hardships I had to overcome at such a young age. I always respond with a smile and share my outlook on that period, which I consider to be one of the happiest of my life: I was living every teenager's dream of not going to school, and still enjoyed a very rich social life. I entertained myself with watching TV and reading books, but I mainly wrote lists. I had so much time on my hands to plan my future. It's a privilege not many enjoy. Our fast-paced schedules prevent most people from even planning their next day.

WHEN I LOOK BACK I CALL THAT PERIOD "THE BEST GIFT I EVER RECEIVED"

Why do I call it a gift? Because at such a young age, I already understood something about the fragility of life, about fate and how it can flip on us just like that. After all, one moment I was a vibrant young man with so many dreams and aspirations, and the next I was paralyzed and in a wheelchair with no clear future ahead. Today I know that these insights normally arrive much later in life, if at all. And although we are surrounded by death, illness, and human tragedies, we do not really grasp the fragility of life until disaster knocks on our door.

Sometimes we even miss the insights and mental gifts handed to us by our very own lives and circumstances. For example, I have a forty-five-year-old acquaintance who managed to survive two cancer strikes in ten years. Her cancers were so aggressive she was unable to do anything for months on end.

But despite the fact that this woman is a cancer survivor and is also very respected in her field of work, she is never satisfied with her own achievements. It seems as though she has forgotten the hard times she has been through and goes on about her life in a constant state of discontent—a classic "the grass is always greener next door" syndrome. If she spent less time observing and appraising other people's gardens and invested more time in her own, I have no doubt in my mind she would have a forest there by now, and much more importantly, she would be a much happier person.

During one of our conversations I said to her, "You've beaten cancer twice! Appreciate what you have managed to do!" She heard me but didn't really take in the meaning of what I said. That's when it dawned on me: every person has their own journey to walk. Sometimes in life we are dealt difficult cards, but it is our call how we choose to play them.

In my case, I learned at a very young age about how fickle life can be. When I was finally able to walk again, I looked at my notebook, which was carefully placed in my under-the-bed secret box of notes and love letters, and made up my mind. For as long as I'm here, I will strike while the iron is hot. I will make all my dreams come true.

Yes, all of them. The little ones, the big ones, the grandiose ones. The obtainable ones and even the seemingly unobtainable ones. The overt as well as the secret ones. The serious and silly ones. The courageous and the mundane. The personal and the familial. The local and the global.

I decided that nothing was going to stand in the way of realizing my dreams: not other people's doubts, not financial limitations, and not the rejections I would most likely experience along the way. And I did, over the course of my career, encounter plenty of those, as I'm sure you have too.

I DECIDED THAT I WAS GOING TO LIVE EVERY DAY AS IF IT WAS THE LAST OF MY LIFE

I WAS GOING TO TICK OFF EACH AND EVERY ONE

OF THE TASKS IN MY ENDLESS LIST.

By the way, I have already ticked most of these off:

- ☑ I entered my first relationship as soon as I recovered (and of course, experienced my first romantic kiss!).

- ☑ Just before my eighteenth birthday I flew to London with my grandparents, and it was one of the most magical overseas trips I've had. The three of us enjoy looking at the photos of that trip again and again.

- ☑ I passed my final theatre exam in high school and played a paralyzed soldier. The examiners claimed that my performance was exceptionally believable. If only they knew how I prepared for the role and who was my source of inspiration…

- ☑ After graduating from drama school, I landed a role in a successful Israeli musical.

- ☑ I started working as a reporter for a local newspaper.

- ☑ With the money I earned at my new job I bought a computer.

- ☑ I traveled to the Great Wall of China.

"The best gift I ever received" has bestowed many gifts upon me. In this book I am hoping to pay those gifts forward.

With the help of this book, I am hoping to inspire you to embark on a mental and personal journey that will prove to be a defining moment for you. My wish is that this book will enable you to become more closely acquainted with an outlook on life that has helped me, as well as many others, come to realize our dreams.

I'M A BIG BELIEVER IN OUR ABILITY TO CREATE OUR OWN REALITY, BUT THIS IS NOT A SPIRITUAL BOOK.

THIS IS A PRACTICAL GUIDE THAT AIMS TO SHARE THE STORIES OF MANY PEOPLE AROUND THE WORLD WHO HAVE WRITTEN LISTS AND REALIZED THEIR DREAMS, PEOPLE I'VE MET VIA SOCIAL NETWORKS—MAINLY FACEBOOK. OVER THE PAST FOUR YEARS THEY HAVE SHARED WITH ME MORE THAN 5,000 LISTS. 5,000 INSPIRATIONAL STORIES AND INSIGHTS. 5,000 LIVES.

I CHOSE NOT TO INCLUDE ANY STATISTICS OR STUDIES THAT WILL INDICATE THE POWER OF SOCIAL NETWORKS AND THE IMPACT OF THE INTERNET. AFTER ALL, THIS KIND OF DATA IS PUBLISHED FROM TIME TO TIME AND CAN BE EASILY ACCESSED ONLINE. YOU MAY FIND USEFUL INFORMATION ON THE SUBJECT IN RANDI ZUCKERBERG'S WONDERFUL BOOK *ROAD TO NOWHERE*. ZUCKERBERG IS AN AMERICAN BUSINESSWOMAN. SHE IS FACEBOOK'S FORMER DIRECTOR OF MARKET DEVELOPMENT AND SPOKESPERSON AND THE SISTER OF THE COMPANY'S CO-FOUNDER AND CEO, MARK ZUCKERBERG.

SO LET GO OF YOUR FEARS, PREJUDICES, AND CYNICISM, BUY A NICE NOTEBOOK, AND LET'S START YOUR JOURNEY WITH *THE LIST*.

You should scribble away on a notepad as you read *The List*. Highlight sentences on your Kindle, write lists, notes, and ideas where and when inspiration takes you. Hopefully the book will empower and encourage you to follow your heart and accomplish the dreams you are destined to realize.

It might also inspire you to write a blog or use social networks in a more effective way. Instead of just uploading pictures of yummy desserts or yammering about the weekend, you might become addicted to "listing" or decide on a much-needed career change or a trip around the world.

But more than anything, I hope that by the time you finish reading the book (or maybe even before that) you will already be on the way to realizing at least one dream, if not more, from your forming list.

The very decision to purchase this book, to commit precious time, focus, and invest in yourself is the first step toward self-fulfillment and conquering your personal goals. You are giving yourself a wonderful gift.

EVERY BIG JOURNEY STARTS WITH ONE SMALL STEP.

3 | WHO AM I?

At the time of writing this book I'm thirty-seven years old. I live in Tel Aviv and am the father of two girls, the amazing six-year-old **Shira**, and our baby **Noga**, who has a beautiful smile on her face.

For the past twenty years I have written for various Israeli media agencies and am currently working as an interviewer for *Israel Hayom (Israel Today)* newspaper.

I have published two best-selling novels and my third book is due for release.

As an actor I have appeared in more than 500 episodes of popular TV shows, performed in plays and musicals, and anchored various radio programs.

I own two décor stores and run a website that serves as a cultural discussion platform. I also direct a writing school.

I have traveled all over the world. I climbed the Great Wall of China, watched the Aurora Borealis (the northern lights), wandered the alleys of the City of God (Cidade de Deus) in Rio de Janeiro, Brazil, and climbed all the stairs of the Eiffel Tower.

I have dined with Bruce Willis, had lunch at Juliet Binoche's house, taken a selfie with Jason Alexander, and interviewed many Hollywood actors, from Meryl Streep to Leonardo DiCaprio. I have visited and stayed in castles, palaces, and holiday houses of the rich and the famous all over the world. This is only a partial list.

I recount these achievements not because I want to show off or impress you, but simply because I have crossed off my list almost every dream I had while sitting in that wheelchair. And I'm still generating new dreams and doing everything I can to make them come true.

YOU CAN TOO.

It is not just a slogan. I know many people who found out about the list method and their lives have changed dramatically.

4 | I'M A DREAM WORKER

Most people I've met need definitions and categories in order to file the information in their brain, so I'm often asked questions like: "So what are you, anyway? What's your profession?" and "How do you make a living?"

I used to mumble a response that was most likely related to whatever significant project I was working on at the time.

Time and again I felt uncomfortable in that my work was so diversified and didn't necessarily have one connecting through-line. I was tempted to believe all kinds of advisors, agents, managers, and friends who suggested that the diversity of my professional interests attested to my lack of focus and commitment. I was warned I'd have professional identity and branding problems, that people would find it hard to identify and connect with me.

It didn't really matter how many examples I pulled out; journalists who were also authors, authors who were also businessmen, businessmen who turned to the entertainment business or entertainers who turned to politics. The same worn-out, depleting sentences kept coming up: "They were lucky," "You can do whatever you want when you have a financial backing," and so on and so forth.

Nowadays, when asked what I do for a living, I answer with a tinge of humor: "My job is to realize my dreams." Today I finally understand that my diverse, frenetic line of work has enriched me as a person and as an artist.

Thanks to the work I do, I have developed an extensive professional network that helps me move things along quicker than ever, and a large community of supporters that are my tailwind, who enable me to spread my wings and fly.

When reminded of my first notebook and that pitiful look in my teacher's eyes when I read her my list, I smile. I smile because I overcame my disability and made my dreams come true, in spite of the lack of faith of so many around me.

When I was very young I had no idea what I was going to do when I grew up. Like many kids my age, I dreamed of being a firefighter. Later on I wanted to become an actor or a journalist, but all I heard was that I couldn't make a living in either of these fields and that I'd better find a more serious profession to pursue. To get me started all I had was one small plan: run a weekly calendar. Focus on that week. Look at it every night to see what I needed to do the next day to achieve my goals. That's how I live today; that's how I've always lived.

I live a rich, diverse lifestyle, exactly as I imagined for myself. I have no routine in my life other than the one enormous achievement that I'm extremely proud of:

I take a nap every afternoon. I always have.

THANKS ARE DUE TO THIS SIMPLE TECHNIQUE: WRITING LISTS. IT ONLY REQUIRES PEN AND PAPER, AN OPEN MIND, WILL, FAITH, AND THEN SOME AUDACITY. TODAY I UTILIZE THE POWER OF SOCIAL NETWORKS TO HELP ME SPREAD MY DREAMS ALL OVER THE WORLD.

THANKS TO THE LISTS THAT HAVE BECOME A WAY OF LIFE FOR ME, I HAVE BEEN REWARDED WITH THE GREATEST EXPERIENCES I COULD HAVE ASKED FOR.

I am no coach, nor am I a psychologist. I do not have a degree in behavioral sciences (truth be told, I don't even have a high school diploma). I didn't grow up in a particularly wealthy family nor was I born in Tel Aviv, Israel's center of unlimited opportunities. I also don't have super powers or magic dust that help me realize my dreams.

I was born to what you would call a normal family. My parents divorced when I was seven and I lived with my mother, while my father remarried and then divorced again. I rarely see him. I wasn't the most popular kid in class, nor was I particularly good looking. Far from it. I never got the highest grades, but I always enjoyed great support from my mother and my grandmother, which encouraged me to pursue my dreams no matter what. I also found inspiration my grandfather's heroic World War II stories. Last but not least, I have accumulated an impressive stack of dreams, and piles of papers filled with my lists.

As I said, I continue to write lists incessantly. My desk is covered with notes, scribble-filled notebooks, and colorful Post-It notes. If you looked in my pockets you would most likely find a note in each one.

These are not grocery or to-do lists, but a collection of goals I would like to achieve and dreams I wish to realize. They are a bit like a company's quarterly plans, only these are for my personal life.

What do these lists look like? Can they be read clearly or are they completely unintelligible? Are they filled with deletions and indecision? I must admit the answers are all yes. These lists are a living, breathing organism. They respond to everything that happens to me and around me.

My dreams are not set in concrete. They are something I continuously mold and change, based on my accomplishments as well as setbacks I encounter along the way. Sometimes I just feel like it's time to set new goals and dreams, maybe even raise the bar for myself.

ARE THERE SPECIFIC TIMES FOR WRITING LISTS?

I've noticed that I always write a new list on the eve of my birthday. Another one when I go on my annual vacation, and another one at the end of Yom Kippur (the Jewish Day of Atonement).

I update my lists when I feel personally or professionally stuck, as well as when I feel fatigued or my energy is low. Since I manage to accomplish most of my goals, it's clear to me that I will keep writing lists for years to come. I will also teach my daughters to do the same.

But don't let this long introduction fool you. This book is not about me and the story here is not my story. I wrote this book because I wanted to pass on the message of the list method, via sharing my own personal story and share the social, Internet-based experiment I started in May 2011 titled *The List Blog*.

In retrospect it turned out that thanks to the blog, and with no prior planning, I found myself in the midst of what could be described as a mass experiment, a social research, which drew in more and more participants, all of whom were exposed to the blog; thousands of Internet users across the world, men and women of all ages and from all walks of life.

The blog has helped me to thoroughly research that elusive field of "dream fulfillment." Today, with the perspective of time and experience, I have a deeper understanding of what it is that drives some people to try and achieve the dreams and goals they've listed. Today I can also better understand what prevents people (myself included) from doing so.

We all have dreams but not all of us follow them.

I think I know why.

I think you should know too.

5 | THE LETTER
I SENT MYSELF

A little over five years ago, on the eve of the Day of Atonement, I decided to tidy up my home office. It's a small space but I make a point of spending a few hours of solitude in it every day. It's my time to dream, write, and prepare the weekly interviews for the newspaper I work for. I also need to spend a good chunk of time on Facebook, to meet new list bloggers and extend my social networking activities.

While dusting off a few discarded Ikea storage boxes, one of them fell off the top shelf and its contents cascaded over the floor. I found myself surrounded by piles of papers and colorful notes.

Birthday cards from my thirtieth birthday, pictures I had no album space for, and an old letter addressed to me. I looked at the handwriting and immediately knew: it was a letter I had sent myself.

I remember thinking it was a strange thing to do. I couldn't recall what it was about or why I did it. I opened the sealed envelope and pulled out its contents—it was a list of dreams. I wrote it during an intimate dinner with ten of my closest friends on New Year's Eve. When we finished our meal and were just about tipsy enough, I asked everyone to write a list of dreams and goals for the new year, much like a New Year's resolution list.

We all sat in front of the empty sheet of paper, alone, and began scribbling down our personal lists. When we finished I had asked my friends to share theirs with the rest of us. Although we were a close-knit bunch and we knew almost everything about each other, not everyone felt comfortable sharing their list.

Some said their list was too private and still not specific enough. Others shared only certain parts of their list, and some had no qualms about it and simply read it out. We listened, discussed the lists, and tried to figure out how each of us could help out in making them happen. When we finished I asked everyone to put their list in an envelope, write their address on it, and hand it to me for safekeeping. They did, and then completely forgot about the lists with which they had entrusted me.

As autumn gave way to winter, I sent my friends their lists as a reminder for the coming spring and for new beginnings. The only one I hadn't mailed was my own list. It was left in that box until it literally fell on my head.

I sat at my desk, opened the envelope, and started reading out my list. As I progressed, a strong sense of pride and accomplishment engulfed me.

ALMOST ALL OF MY DREAMS HAD COME TRUE!

OR SHOULD I SAY—I MADE MY DREAMS COME TRUE, WITH MY OWN BARE HANDS.

- ☑ Move to a bigger apartment. I have moved into a place that is double the size of the apartment I had before and there is even a small garden. (On my next list I should write a note on spending more time cultivating it.)
- ☑ Have another baby. We have a six-month-old baby girl!
- ☑ Publish a book. I have published two best-selling novels. The rights for one of the books were sold to a production company who wanted to develop it as a TV series.
- ☑ Perform in the theatre. At the time I was acting in a fringe show called *Shufra* which has had considerable success in both Israel and New York. It also toured a few international fringe festivals.
- ☑ Establish a business. I was in the midst of opening a store, called MADE IN TLV, which is located at the trendy old railway complex in Neveh Tzedek. It specializes in locally designed crafts and décor products that pay tribute to the city of Tel Aviv.

I wondered how it happened that I had executed almost every item on that list, despite having completely forgotten I'd ever written it!

Only three items stood between me and my complete self-fulfillment:

☐ Take painting lessons. I never did.

☐ Learn French. I started but I quit after a few weeks because it clashed with my TV series shooting days (I guess I'm also really good at giving myself excuses).

☐ Go to the gym.

I bet you good money that you are all acquainted with the last item on my list. Most of us long to be healthier, thinner, and better looking. For twenty years now (!) I've been shuffling this particular item along from one list to the next, while promising myself that I would finally get my act together and do it. I'd subscribe to the new, funky gym in town, then forget about it and pass the membership on to a friend. I had spent so much money on memberships I never used I was practically a philanthropist of Tel Aviv gyms.

I read back the list and wondered how it could be that everything that society deems "difficult" I've managed to accomplish, things like setting up a business or writing a book, while ignoring the simplest, most mundane items?

What actually prevented me from going to the gym? Why didn't I take painting lessons? I've painted in the past and wasn't half bad at it, so what happened?

I had the whole of the Day of Atonement, which is traditionally a solemn, quiet day, to think about it. I shared the question with my family, as well as my Facebook friends. The question I posted was, "Why have I not been able to be consistent in going to the gym?" The answers poured in. But hang on—before I tell you what they were, take a minute to write down for yourself what you think the answers could be.

? | EXERCISE

? What, in your opinion, makes people realize certain dreams, while shelving others?

? What makes or helps you realize certain dreams, while other dreams that are equally important to you don't materialize?

? What is the one item you shuffle along from one list to the next? (What, you don't have a list yet?!)

WHY I HAVE NOT BEEN GOING TO THE GYM?
NON RESEARCH-BASED, YET INTERESTING ANSWERS.

"You didn't really want to go to the gym. The things you really wanted to accomplish you followed wholeheartedly," a Facebook friend had responded.

I wrote back: "Call me superficial, but losing a few extra kilos is just as important to me as starring in a new play, publishing a book, or increasing my annual income. Not only is it important to me personally, but professionally as well."

"Who likes gyms?" someone else wrote me, who, judging by his photo, goes to one very often.

"It's probably hard for you to commit to long-term efforts," a friend told me.

"But I can sit for two years and work on a book! My computer is always in my bag and I use every free moment to write." I completely rejected his analysis.

"A book is a very rewarding undertaking, accompanied by money and fame", he insisted.

"A skinny, attractive body is also very rewarding," I answered. "Besides, you must have never seen an Israeli author's royalty check if you think writing a book is in any way financially rewarding."

I didn't get a single satisfying answer that would ease my mind and solve the mystery, so I decided to research what it is that really prevents us from realizing our dreams. I published the question on my Facebook page and the answers were fascinating to say the least.

WHAT IS PREVENTING US FROM REALIZING ALL OF OUR DREAMS?

✔ It's hard for us to do things that are not in our comfort zone.

✔ We have a limited amount of energy; we can't do everything.

✔ It's a matter of priorities.

✔ If we fulfill all our dreams now, we will have nothing to aspire to. We need unfulfilled dreams to motivate us forward.

✔ We are afraid to fail; if we fail it might discourage us altogether.

✔ Our fear of success or change stops us from realizing some of our dreams.

✔ When we face our biggest desires we naturally push aside smaller, more mundane desires and aspirations.

✔ I have many dreams but I'm very young. People will ridicule me if they hear about my big ambitions.

✔ I'm eighty-seven years old. I have seen everything and done everything. I have no dreams left.

✔ We invest so much mental energy into our big dreams that the little ones are often left behind.

✔ It's a matter of passion.

✔ Laziness and procrastination.

Examining this list of possible explanations, all I see is a list of excuses, namely time and money. The very same excuses I use in moments of weakness, despite my awareness of my dreams and goal.

True, our time is limited, but surveys continuously suggest we spend so much time watching TV and losing ourselves in social networks. In fact, if we were to restrict our TV/computer usage by merely one day per week, we would have already gained a few valuable hours in our jam-packed weekly schedules.

I also reject the money excuse. It's true that not all of us are rich and many of us struggle to make ends meet on a monthly basis, but realizing our dreams is not a privilege reserved for the wealthy.

There is no doubt about it: financial backing is needed in order to achieve our grandest dreams. A road trip in New Zealand, for example, will cost thousands of dollars and will be a great strain on the family budget. But most of our dreams are smaller and only require a feasible financial investment. Things like buying new clothes every now and then, refurbishing our bathroom, or buying a reclining armchair are reasonable expenses.

What stands between us and making our dreams happen is mainly poor financial planning, lack of determination and audacity, and inaccurate estimation of our financial situation by an amount of money that is anywhere between a few hundreds and a few thousands of dollars a year. This is the kind of money that is obtainable through smart financial self-handling. A short-term savings plan, a small loan from the bank, help from family and friends, and, in the spirit of contemporary culture crowdfunding campaigns via recognized websites.

OVER THE PAST FEW YEARS I HAVE MET THOUSANDS OF DREAMERS. MOST OF THEM HAD HUMBLE, ACHIEVABLE GOALS THAT, APART FROM WILL AND DETERMINATION, MAINLY REQUIRE WISE FINANCIAL PLANNING OR A CONVERSATION WITH THE BANK ADVISOR. DREAMING OF GETTING A RECREATIONAL PILOT'S LICENSE, CLIMBING MOUNT KILIMANJARO, OR HAVING A FRONT ROW SEAT AT A BEYONCÉ CONCERT? THESE ARE ALL EASILY OBTAINABLE.

MAKING A DREAM COME TRUE MAY ONLY COST A FEW HUNDRED DOLLARS, BUT THE FEELING OF MISSING OUT ON THINGS THAT ARE IMPORTANT TO US IS FAR MORE COSTLY.

6 | FANTASIES
DO COME TRUE

Some dreams are rock solid. Some are latent. Some roll off the line quicker than a race car and some are still vacuum-sealed and we have no idea when we will air them out.

Our job is to be attentive and alert, recognize their potential at the right moment, and know when to spark them off.

When I read the newspaper's financial section, I get very excited about the opening of small businesses, particularly those born out of one person's vision. A brilliant little idea turned into a viable business.

I'm particularly excited by concept stores, both in Israel and abroad, which clearly reflect the owner's dream and vision. A few examples come to mind: one is a tiny little store in Tel Aviv that has been turned into a public dog shower for pet owners who prefer the messiness of pet showering outside of their bathroom (how did I not think of this myself?). The birthday store in Tel Aviv's CBD, the used clothes and books store that is also a café, or the $2 café chain.

Last year I met a great couple through *The List* project and we have become good friends. Thanks to them, I rediscovered the extent to which necessity is the mother of invention and how important it is to listen to your heart and follow your dreams.

These two have turned their lives around by developing an application for toddlers where they can watch animals, musical instruments, and vehicles, explore the sounds they produce, and even memorize their names. Their app rates highly on the world's popular app list and provides them with an extremely high monthly income.

This is a couple who until two years ago were stuck knee-deep in debt and could barely make ends meet. You cannot imagine the negative responses they received when they first shared their app idea. They were told that they were wasting their time and were scorned for spending what little money they had on an expensive computer needed to develop their idea. They both had children from previous relationships as well as a new baby together. Those negative responses could have easily driven them down the beaten track of excuses (no time, no money, etc) but instead they chose to follow their dream and realize their vision: develop a successful app against all odds. Today they are well on their way to becoming millionaires.

I asked them to tell me their story so that I can share it here, to motivate and inspire people. Their names are Eran and Lia and this is their story:

Some people can lie to themselves their whole life and suppress feelings of frustration. Unfortunately, I was not blessed with that ability. If I don't pursue my dreams in my waking hours, they come back to haunt me at night.

I had always dreamed of getting out of the rat race. I'm a musician who has worked in IT for most of my life. For years on end I found myself staring at a computer screen at work, while my soul was at home in front of the piano. I could see my days wasting away. As time went by, it was harder and harder for me to hide it. I was running late for work in the morning and would leave earlier than everyone else to go home. Until one day, for the first time in my life, I was fired from my job. In the absence of any financial safety net, I started sending my CV around in the hope of finding myself a new "jail" that would pay for my precious time but my lack of ambition just grew bigger and bigger. I remember a job interview where I was asked to perform a computer task as a test but instead of getting right on it and facing the challenge, I got up and left the interview.

My employment terms got shorter and shorter. During my last job, Lia, my wife, opened a savings account and surprised me with tickets to Amsterdam. We didn't really hit the museums or anything like that. We mainly lay in our hotel room and did a lot of thinking, pondering, and staring at the ceiling fan. I told Lia about Steve Jobs, who had just invented the iPhone and opened a virtual store where anybody could upload an app and sell it to iPhone users all around the world. Apple takes only thirty percent of the income and the rest goes to the programmer.

As soon as Lia heard that, she knew we were going to be millionaires. Honestly, it seemed a little farfetched to me. I didn't have a Mac computer or the money to buy one and I didn't have an idea for an app. Oh, I also didn't know how to program or have the time to learn.

To understand why Lia knew they were going to be millionaires, we need to go back to her childhood and trace her thinking patterns. Here is what she told me:

Ever since I was very young, I knew I needed freedom. Freedom from bosses and nine-to-five commitments, freedom to control my own time, financial freedom, and the freedom to take a siesta every day. After getting divorced, I had to raise two girls on my own. I found myself working two jobs, sometimes even three, while being a full-time mum in the afternoons and evenings. Ever since I was a little girl, I've been writing in a diary and every once in a while, I write all sorts of lists—decisions, goals, dreams. When I met Eran, I discovered that he also had a list of dreams, just like mine. That was one of the things that brought us together.

Eran continues:

Lia convinced me to take a loan and buy a new Mac and somehow we did it. A friend at work told me about a free video online: a course on developing iOS 7 Apps for iPhone and iPad that was guided by Apple engineers and delivered by Stanford University.

I downloaded the first lesson and didn't understand a thing. I had worked with computers but had never written a program. I watched the same video over and over again, stopping and starting every few minutes to make sure I wasn't missing anything. I told myself that anything is possible, including this. I convinced myself not to give up and that I would eventually get it.

The first lesson, which was only an hour long, took me a whole week. I studied day and night. I watched the videos over and over again, pulling out my hair and then re-starting. This is what I did for two solid months and by then, I was almost halfway through the course. That was when I lost my job.

According to everyone around me, I was supposed to be looking for a job. I was living on welfare benefits, money was running low, and debts started to accumulate. People told me that apps were not a good investment, that I was stupid, irresponsible, off with the fairies. You want to know what I did? I put all of my eggs in one basket and prayed they would eventually hatch.

One day, I saw our toddler looking at a children's book that had animal illustrations in it. I was appalled. The cow didn't look like a cow, the dog looked like a cloud and the rest of the animals were drawn in an abstract manner. I was mortified that my child might think that this is how these animals actually look and took away the book. That night I woke up with an idea—design an app that would show children real pictures of animals. A child using this app would no longer have incorrect ideas of how these animals looked. I could also attach sound to each picture. Each picture would contain the animal's name and make the appropriate sound of the creature in it.

That was going to be our app. I felt really good about this idea.

I put my head back on the pillow but before falling asleep I realized that I might not remember anything in the morning. Unwillingly I got out of bed, found a pen and paper, scribbled down the idea, and went back to sleep. During the night, I woke up several times with ideas for different apps, one that showed children images of vehicles and another showing children musical instruments. I woke up in the morning with only a vague memory of having had an idea. It's a good thing I'd written it all down.

When I reread my ideas I immediately understood that they were actually one app that presented pictures and sounds. This didn't require complex programming, so I was able to write it in only two days. After three more months of searching for the right pictures and processing the sounds, the app was ready. All we had left to do was find a good name for it; eventually we decided on calling it *Sound Touch.*

We released our app at the end of December 2009 and the first two months were a total disappointment. We averaged two downloads a day which paid a dollar-and-a-half—even the tooth fairy is more generous than that! Then one day, two months after our first app-store appearance, there were 500 downloads! The next day there were over 600! We couldn't understand it. A short inquiry revealed that Apple had decided to feature us in the "New and Recommended" list. Our app is currently one of the most successful in the world with over two million users purchasing it. It's available in more than thirty languages and usually rates five stars out of five. It's being used by professionals in the fields of speech therapy, autism, hearing disabilities, blindness, and even adults with dementia.

The money that's coming from Apple every month is enabling me to finally play, create, and develop, and Lia can now dedicate herself to writing and to her other hobbies. I don't even have to work all the time. My "store" is open for business 24/7 and I'm at home enjoying myself.

Lia adds:

We have achieved the freedom to work the hours that suit us—even when we're asleep or on vacation we make money. When someone earns even one dollar while they are asleep, they understand the power that comes with the ability to "multiply time." We all have twenty-four hours but how many of them can we actually work? Twelve? But if you sell even while you're asleep, you multiply your work hours by millions and gain freedom. Our company is basically two people who conveniently work at home.

"THE PEOPLE WHO ARE CRAZY ENOUGH TO THINK THEY CAN CHANGE THE WORLD ARE THE ONES WHO DO."

STEVE JOBS

7 | A DREAM'S
BUILDING BLOCKS
(OR: A STORE THAT WAS BORN ON A PILLAR)

The Internet is full of stories about courageous people who have decided to pursue their dreams and not let people's disapproval stand in their way.

For example, Marine Sgt. **Scott Moore** was stationed in Afghanistan in 2011 and had the dream of meeting **Mila Kunis**. He uploaded an eighteen-second clip to YouTube, inviting her to the 236 years of Marine Corps' celebration ball. The film went viral with more than four million hits. Kunis, of course, immediately RSVP'd for this much-desired date with Moore.

Yoni Bloch (an Israeli singer), also quite the dream maker, has revealed in interviews how his life changed thanks to the website New Stage, an online platform where he published songs he had written. The songs became a success and were passed around until they reached the daughter of the CEO of the Israeli record label NMC. She passed them onto her father and Yoni's musical career was launched.

Another Israeli dreamer is **Eliyahu Loev**, who in 2010 decided to establish an original advertising agency named hultzut.com (shirts. com). His idea was as simple as it was original: every day he would take his own picture wearing a shirt with his sponsor's logo, turn this picture into his Facebook profile picture, and upload a correlating video clip. The pricing of this original publicity was also unique and funny: the first day would cost $1, second day $2, third day $3, and so on, until the last day of the year would cost $365. Within a few days the project spread through the various media platforms and Loev had rapidly sold thousands of dollars' worth of "advertising space."

Kyle MacDonald, a young blogger from Canada, is another Internet success story. He started a website called One Red Paperclip in which he had suggested that people barter his red paper clip. His goal was to keep exchanging goods until he had bartered a house. His first barter was for a fish-shaped pen. He bartered that for a hand-sculpted doorknob, which he then bartered for a Coleman camp stove. The stove was exchanged for a Honda generator, which in turn was bartered for an "instant party" package consisting of an empty keg and an IOU for filling the keg with beer. The next exchange was a snowmobile for a two-person trip to Yahk, British Columbia. A cube van was exchanged for a recording contract with Metalworks in Mississauga, Ontario. A year's rent in Phoenix, Arizona was bartered for one afternoon with **Alice Cooper.** A **KISS** motorized snow globe for a role in the film *Donna on Demand*, and finally, after only fourteen trades, Kyle MacDonald was given a two-story farmhouse in Kipling, Saskatchewan. He then published a book about his project. I think it's safe to assume that the royalties from his book helped furnish his new home.

In Kyle MacDonald's case this was a fruitful Internet game, with zero expenses or risks (excluding the potential for public humiliation). Clearly, not every idea will work. You need luck and good timing and you need to be attentive to the zeitgeist of the time. If you want something badly enough nothing can stand in your way. I have proof of it hanging on a pillar in the middle of my living room. No, I do not carve totem poles as a hobby—I just work at realizing my dreams.

☑

Six years ago I went to Amsterdam on a vacation with friends. In one of the many souvenir shops on Kalverstraat, the city's main street for shopping, I bought a tourist souvenir. It was a long clear plastic sheet divided into twenty pockets. Each pocket featured a black and white postcard of one of the city's famous sites.

In my old 1940s apartment in Tel Aviv, there is an ugly column right in the middle of the living room. It reminds me of the pillars in old theatres that in London often block your view. To decorate this atrocity, I thought it would be nice to put postcards of Tel Aviv in the plastic pockets. When I returned home I spent two whole weeks sifting through postcards of the White City (a part of Tel Aviv famous for its Bauhaus architecture on UNESCO's World Heritage list) but found nothing. I rummaged through old bookshops but all I found were terrible postcards from the eighties, a camel near a pay phone, a girl in a bikini eating watermelon with the word Shalom (Hebrew for "hello" and also "peace") above her in bold, or a bad photo of a mundane street captioned "A night in Tel Aviv."

Is this what tourists take home from Israel? At first it made me laugh but then it actually upset me. As if Israel doesn't have enough PR issues already. As if it's not enough that in some places people think Israelis ride camels to work and to school—why was there no contemporary imagery of Tel Aviv?

Necessity is the mother of all invention, right? So I took my camera and wandered the city streets taking good quality photos I could use to cover our living room pillar. I developed thirty of them in black and white, placed them in the plastic pockets, and was finally at peace with the pillar.

Visitors to my house were impressed by my little piece of home décor and wanted to know where I had bought it. By the fiftieth compliment I'd realized that what worked in Amsterdam would work just as well in Tel Aviv. Tel Aviv is a city loved by many locals and tourists alike and if New Yorkers, Parisians, and Londoners show off their cities, we can too. Even if we don't have a grand monument such as the Leaning Tower of Pisa, the Eiffel Tower, or London's Big Ben.

Looking at the pillar from top to bottom, I had an epiphany—just as the Brits have a mug or a plate with the queen's portrait on it and the Americans fly the Star Spangled Banner on every pole they can get their hands on, it was time for Tel Avivians to proudly present a chic magnet of Rothschild Boulevard on their fridge.

This is how a twenty-euro souvenir from Amsterdam sparked my imagination and a new décor store was born. I called it Made In TLV, a store featuring Tel Aviv–themed artifacts, produced in Tel Aviv by Tel Aviv artists and designers.

I must admit, back in those days I had no experience in managing a business whatsoever—I could barely manage my invoice book—but I was determined to get the ball rolling and looked for people who could help me realize my dream.

I met businessmen and influential Tel Avivians, all of whom had significant accomplishments attached to their name. They all thought it was a stupid idea. "What are you going to sell? Musical mugs shaped like the Agam fountain in Dizengoff Square? Paddles? (a very popular game on the Tel Aviv beach)." "If such a store doesn't exist, it's probably because there's no demand for it," said an owner of a well-known Tel Aviv brand name, who until then I had perceived to be a visionary man. Instead I discovered a well-off man who had achieved all of his dreams, to the point of not dreaming anymore. What's worse is that he started to belittle other people's dreams.

No matter what the responses were, I continued to shout my dream louder and louder until I met someone who thought my idea was interesting and could even be profitable. We decided to go for it and scheduled an appointment with a business consultant. At the meeting the consultant listened as we outlined all the information, made some calculations, and eventually came up with the figure we needed to make this dream happen—ILS 250,000 (around US$70,000). In other words, my dream's price tag was quarter of a million shekels.

REMINDER: TIME AND MONEY ARE THE TWO MOST COMMON DREAM DESTROYERS THAT (MENTALLY) PREVENT US FROM GOING AFTER OUR DREAMS.

The lack of money threatened to turn the lights off on my dream and leave it lying on the "rehearsal room floor."

8 | LIFE IS A GAME
(OR: A FATEFUL MEETING WITH AN ATTENTIVE BANKER)

When the meeting finished, my business partner and I stayed in the café and started doing the math. Both of us together could barely scrape ILS50,000 toward our new décor store; how on earth would we come up with 200,000 more?

We applied for a loan from all of the major banks only to have all of our applications rejected, regardless of our financial history. It was 2009 and the global recession was reaching Israel. The banks didn't want to fund unnecessary adventures with people who couldn't demonstrate sufficient business management experience. Unable to secure substantial financial support, my dream was getting further away, laminated in a clear plastic cover on an ugly pillar.

One day, my business partner and I were walking down Rothschild Avenue in Tel Aviv, where the major banks' headquarters are situated, and noticed there was one we hadn't tried yet! We ran into the building, focused all of our strength and enthusiasm, pulled out our presentation (I always carry my laptop with me), and gave a passionate speech about our idea to a very attentive banker.

When we finished she smiled at us and said, "Look, it's very brave of you. You are trying to do something that hasn't been done in Tel Aviv before but I love your determination and enthusiasm. Let me see what I can do for you."

Fifteen minutes later we had an approved loan. No collateral and no co-signatures required. The loan was approved on the basis of our idea and enthusiasm, thanks to one attentive banker who had agreed to think outside the box.

We were lucky enough to meet this specific banker who had an open mind and a sharp sense for business. This is exactly what Seneca, the Roman philosopher, said: "Luck is what happens when preparation meets opportunity. So when opportunity knocks, you have to be prepared to open the door."

The loan was spread over five years with a reasonable monthly return. We planned it so that even in the worst-case scenario, where no tourist out of the millions who flood Israel each year would walk into our store, we would still be able to pay it back. Each partner would have to pay about ILS2,000 a month for the remaining amortization period. It's not a small amount, but it's not the kind of money that will send a working person into bankruptcy. If you give up eating out and other little luxuries you could meet the target. Anyway, when you open a new business, these are the kinds of things you should expect to forgo in the pursuit of your dream.

In an interview for a financial TV magazine, I was asked why I wasn't afraid to gamble so much money on a first business, especially considering I came from the arts world. I told the reporter that my beloved late grandmother, a great influence in my life, bought a lottery ticket once a week for forty years. She never won but it didn't stop her from investing an astronomical amount of money in her dream of becoming a millionaire. Instead of buying lottery tickets for twenty years, I play with one big ticket.

LIFE (AND SUCCESSFUL PEOPLE I HAVE MET ALONG THE WAY) HAVE TAUGHT ME THAT IF YOU TAKE A RISK YOU MAY LOSE, BUT YOU MAY ALSO WIN BIG

We signed the papers and went on our way with enough money in our pockets to realize the dream: our store, Made In TLV.

Made In TLV received a lot of media coverage both in Israel and abroad. Tourists and local Tel Aviv lovers raided our shelves and fairly quickly we received franchise requests for the concept. The store has been running successfully for over four years.

Why am I sharing this story with you? Because most of the average dreams I encounter require less money than that dream we had. They often require smaller amounts that can be raised through family and friends, a small loan from the bank, or even crowdfunding campaigns via websites such as Kickstarter.

IN THE ERA WE LIVE IN, **TIME AND MONEY—** THE MOST COMMON OBSTACLES ON OUR WAY TO REALIZING **OUR DREAM**—HAVE BECOME EASIER TO SURPASS. ALL WE HAVE TO DO IS TRAIN OUR "COURAGE MUSCLES" AND JUMP OVER THE BAR.

9 HOW I FOUND
JOHN AMAECHI

One evening, around the time I found an envelope containing my original list, I was watching Oprah interview **John Amaechi,** a former NBA player who had recently published a revealing biography where he came out as gay. The interview was fascinating and I found Amaechi's story intriguing and very brave. After the interview was over, I still had so many questions I wanted to ask Amaechi, so I decided I had to contact him. Only I had no idea how to reach him.

"Perhaps via this new Facebook website everyone is joining," I thought to myself and I quickly set up my new profile and started searching for Amaechi's. I got about thirty results—most of them were fake profiles carrying only his picture. I befriended each profile and waited to be approved. Some of the profiles seemed real but then proved to be fake. Others didn't seem very reliable and some were completely inactive. One of the profiles had a few albums in it, an impressive amount of friends and ample activity. I found albums of pool parties and barbeque dinners that seemed completely authentic. My mission was complete.

I'D FOUND JOHN AMAECHI!

I wrote him a short private message about his interview on **Oprah** and how it had left me with some questions that I would love to ask him. He replied the next day and we became Facebook friends. Years later when writing an article about inspirational people, John kindly agreed to be interviewed.

The fact that it took me less than twenty-four hours to contact an international basketball star resonated and made me realize how small our world has actually become.

Every person can be contacted by clicking the mouse, if not directly then via an assistant, PR person, publisher, or someone close.

This is how I managed to contact someone who was close to Madonna asking her for an interview (she refused). I have also contacted senior business people in Israel and abroad and many influential people in the entertainment and media world. Some of them have helped promote my professional aspirations.

SO WHAT'S STRONGER? THE HESITATION THAT KEEPS US FROM REALIZING OUR DREAMS, OR THE IMPULSE THAT PUSHES US FORWARD DESPITE THE RISKS? THIS IS EXACTLY WHERE MY INTERNET EXPERIMENT COMES IN. IT PROVED BEYOND A REASONABLE DOUBT WHAT I ALREADY KNEW: TODAY, IN THE EXCITING TECHNOLOGICAL ERA WE LIVE IN, A FEW GOOGLE SEARCHES AND THE CLICK OF A MOUSE CAN SIGNIFICANTLY ADVANCE US TOWARD OUR GOALS.

10 | THE LIST
BLOG

In May 2011, I wrote a new list of limitless dreams and goals, published it to my blog and on social networks, and forwarded it to as many people as possible. I was curious to know how far my post would go, much like sending a letter in a bottle—you never know where it's going to end up. I wrote the blog in English as well as in Hebrew to increase my chances of success and to reach out to as many potential supporters in our global village as possible.

I paid a graphic designer to design my Wordpress blog and uploaded my own private list, including ten things I wanted to achieve in the following 400 days.

Why 400 days? It was an arbitrary choice. The number just popped into my head and had a nice ring to it. I figured it was enough time to accomplish the goals I had set myself.

This is the list I posted:

☐ Develop a "six-pack" belly.

☐ Be interviewed on French television, but learn to speak French first.

☐ Complete my high school studies and sit the final exams.

☐ Rehabilitate a homeless person.

☐ Establish an international society for children.

☐ Interview Oprah who is my inspiration and have the interview broadcast on her TV channel.

☐ Travel around Australia without spending a single dollar.

☐ Sell a television format based on the idea of *The List*, preferably at the Cannes TV festival.

☐

☐

You may have noticed that two are missing. I decided to leave two blank spots for dreams that I hadn't thought of yet.

In my post I wrote that whoever helped me achieve my goals would receive my help with their list in return.

I believe in mutual help. I have a vision of a world filled with list writers and dreamers who help each other, a world in which everyone is happy to take small measures to help someone else. I have no doubt that humanity would be happier and more fulfilled in such a world, motivated by the joy that is derived from helping others.

IMAGINE A WORLD WHERE LEADERS PUBLISH LISTS OF ANNUAL GOALS FOR THEIR ADMINISTRATIONS AND FOLLOW THESE LISTS IN FULL TRANSPARENCY. IMAGINE A WORLD WHERE WE KNOW WHAT OUR LEADERS ARE DOING AND WHERE THEY ARE TAKING US. THERE'S AN IDEA FOR YOU... SOUNDS UTOPIAN? IT COULD BE OUR REALITY.

The different items on my list were not caprice—they were very well reasoned.

For example, I'm totally capable of financing my own trip to Australia but I wanted to challenge myself to see if I could do it without investing so much as one dollar into it. I really wanted to find out how far my will-power would take me and to discover how the world would react to such a challenge.

The desire to rehabilitate a homeless person is the echo of a distant memory. A homeless person once approached me in the street asking for money. I gathered my courage and asked him what drove him to such miserable circumstances. He told me his stepfather had thrown him out of home, so I decided to help him—instead of simply giving him a coin and moving on, I offered to help him rebuild his life. We arranged to meet at the same place the following day.

We met the following day, even though neither of us was sure the other would turn up.

We applied for an ID card so that he could receive government benefits. After running from one ministry to another and finally finding him a bed to sleep on, we started to hunt for a job. For six weeks I thought my plans were succeeding, but then one day he disappeared and never came back to meet me.

I continued to look for him and almost every day I found myself at our meeting spot, but it was all in vain. I felt a real sense of failure. Over time this turned into a strong desire to help another homeless person and this time succeed in helping them get back on their feet.

Meeting Oprah has been one of my dreams since my days in the wheelchair. I love watching her show and draw strength from her interviews. Her optimism and her healthy approach to life have influenced me and strengthened my desire to empower others. For this I want to meet her and thank her. I also want to share with her the new insights I have gained from the List blog, so that she can pass them to others via her website, magazine, and TV channel.

I know I will reach her. It's as clear to me as the sun in the sky.

"YOU HAVE TO TRY THE IMPOSSIBLE TO ACHIEVE THE POSSIBLE."
HERMANN HESSE

What would Hesse have written had he lived today, in an era where everything seems possible?

11 | HANGING ON TO THIN
AIR

I published my blog on a Thursday evening.

I was so excited. I copied the link to my first post and published it on my Facebook page. The next morning I checked the web counter and saw 500 blog hits.

I actually wasn't that impressed and started berating myself—I have 5,000 Facebook friends and more followers on top; a mere 10 percent was a disappointment. But the following day the blog started to pick up speed. The amount of shares grew rapidly and by the end of the first week I had received 5,000 blog hits. Hundreds of site visitors were leaving enthusiastic and supportive responses, while others preferred to private-message me.

Within two weeks the web counter had already registered an impressive 20,000 visitors and by the end of the first month the blog had 50,000 visits from all over the world, including Jordan, Australia, and Russia.

As the amount of shares continued to grow, the responses on the blog accumulated and the media started calling. The interviewer became an interviewee. I found myself on morning shows and answering questions on leading websites. People wanted to understand the idea behind the experiment and whether I intended to check off all the dreams published on the blog.

EVERY NEW WEBSITE VISITOR OR POST SHARE
BROADENED MY CIRCLE AND HELPED ME TAKE BIGGER, W I D E R STEPS.

The media showed great interest my dream of a "six-pack" and cynically dismissed the possibility that I would actually manage to achieve any of the other goals. Their skepticism didn't discourage me.

I PUT A LOT OF ENERGY INTO PROMOTING THE WHOLE LIST IDEA—NOT JUST MY GOALS, BUT EVERYONE ELSE'S, TOO. AT THIS STAGE I DIDN'T REALIZE THAT WHAT I WAS GOING TO ACHIEVE AND DISCOVER ON THIS JOURNEY WOULD BE MUCH BIGGER THAN ANY PERSONAL ACHIEVEMENT.

12 | THE WORLD RESPONDS
TO MY LIST

The first direct response I received to my list was an email that came all the way from Chicago less than a week after my blog went online. It was from an Israeli woman, now living in Chicago, telling me of a family connection who worked at **Oprah's** studio. "Here's the studio's address, and here's her home address (one of her homes). Write to her and tell her your story."

A woman from New York wrote to me explaining, "I once met Oprah and we have a few mutual acquaintances. I'll try to connect the two of you."

Two days later I got another email: "I know one of Oprah's producers. His name is Don and here is his email. Write to him." So I did.

An Israeli living in New York read about my dream of a six-pack stomach and sent a link with information on a DVD made by a hard-core trainer with the perfect six-pack stomach. "Order his DVD set. It really works," he wrote.

"They don't ship to Israel," I wrote to him.

"You know what? I'll buy the DVD for you as a present and mail it to you," he replied.

Other readers, responding to my idea of "mutual help," volunteered to translate the blog into other languages. Posts have now been translated to French, German, Russian, and even Persian.

I was overwhelmed by the kindness and generosity of people and that was just the beginning.

WHEN A TSUNAMI COMES YOU CAN'T HELP BUT GET WET...

I was contacted by a the man in charge of the PR for Holmes Place, a luxurious chain of gyms:

"Health and toning are our top priorities. We want to offer you a free gym membership for the full duration of your experiment: 400 days. We would also like to offer you a personal trainer and a dietitian. Just come and exercise."

I never took him up on his offer, despite how fantastic their gyms and swimming pools are. I just wasn't ready yet (you have to admit you haven't heard that one before).

I did respond to an extremely generous personal trainer who wrote to me about an American running method called "fun running." Even though this sounded like a total oxymoron—how could the word "fun" be connected with "running"?—I did like the sound of it and decided to give it a chance. I started to enjoy my runs on Tel Aviv's sandy beaches. I improved my cardiovascular endurance and lost eleven pounds. Eventually I ran away from the trainer—I guess I still have my athletic limitations.

A generous computer programmer, living in the north of Israel, wrote to me: "Your blog and the idea behind it are great; however, can I suggest a few improvements? Any new application you wish to add, just say the word and I will do it, for free." I was overwhelmed. A programmer costs at least $100 per hour, and here was this guy, offering me his help for free.

People emailed me from Australia offering me a spare bed in their guest rooms or in their lounge rooms. Within a few weeks I had accumulated thirty accommodation invitations in Australia—the farthest place I had ever dreamed of visiting and all free of charge. All I had to take care of was my $2,000 plane ticket. Surprisingly (or not), the one item I thought would take the longest was the one I was the closest to checking off.

But the best was yet to come. When it did, it was in a red sports car, driven by a charming monk.

Two weeks after *The List* blog was published online, I happened to interview **Robin Sharma** (the author of international best-seller, *The Monk Who Sold his Ferrari*) for *Israel Hayom (Israel Today)*, the newspaper I work for.

At the end of our transatlantic phone call I told him about my blog. He asked to read it so I sent him a link. In return, I received an article from him about the inspirational story of the founder of the Four Seasons hotel chain. The article was about realizing dreams and Sharma asked me to publish it in Hebrew. You can find it on my blog.

Odetta Danin, Israel's first lady of life-style and a homemaking guru, also came across my blog. We started a nightly correspondence about the road to achieving dreams and two weeks later, this legendary woman wrote her whole weekly column in the spirit of my blog.

Here are Odetta's thoughts about achieving your dreams and setting goals, as originally published in *Ma'ariv* newspaper on May 13, 2011:

HOW TO ACCOMPLISH WHAT YOU WANT
(And: a great idea on how to stop gaining weight)

Hello friends!

I have a cute Facebook friend who is just addicted to ticking goals off his list. He sets himself daily, monthly and annual goals, and then goes on to achieve them. His achievement list (as well as the list of unachieved goals), is endless.

My friend has some kind of bulimia. It's not a food-related bulimia, but rather a "life bulimia." The guy is like a Queen song. Don't stop him now, he's having such a good time, he's having a ball, and he wants it all, and he wants it NOW!

My personal little take on the subject is that there's nothing wrong with his list of goals, just mind the dosage. From my point of view, excessive dosage works the same way sex addiction does: so much sex (achievements) and still the addict is never satisfied and is doomed to try and repeat the act over and over again just for the sake of experiencing those seconds of glorious feeling. How else is he going to catch it by the tail? It will never mean anything because every use of drugs is like buying clothes when you're thirsty. A truck full of clothes will not quench thirst. In this case, the proof is in the pudding: if you don't have time to lay back and enjoy the fruits of your labor, beep beep, you have to tick off the next destination; there is no contentment or gratification. I know that many life coaches are now raising their batons to hit me on the head because according to them, we must worship the idea of ambitiousness, but that's just it—we don't!

WHY CERTAIN DREAMS DON'T COME TRUE.

My friend always complains about putting off two or three things for the next list. For years, he's been promising himself that "one day" he will get lean and toned and learn French and he really can't understand how it is that those things are not happening for him. He has lifted bigger loads, managed to execute much bigger plans, so why is it not working here? And my answer is simple: he cannot find the strength or ability in himself for some things (assuming they are not impossible for him on account of some psychological entanglement or deep secret aspects of his personality), because he refuses to accept the verdict, which is the simplest truth: that he really couldn't care less about sit-ups or conjugating verbs in French. Très simple. However, he really likes the "French Apollo" image and would to see himself in it. Well, he likes it, he truly does, but not enough to make himself sweat over it. What can you do? Sometimes a fact is just a fact.

THE IMPORTANCE OF THE RIGHT WILL.

My friend's mother, **Yona Brener**, used to say that "will is a talent" whenever she wanted to explain how a certain "good for nothing" has managed to reach the top. Of course, she was right because "will" is the master engine that governs all the other engines we know. In the race toward achievement, will is the ace that wins over wisdom, money, pedigree, beauty, education, talent and all the rest of those virtues with which we usually gauge success. It is the wonderful resource that handicapped people like Professor Stephen Hawking use in order to write best sellers using their left eyelash, and in its absence, even completely healthy people will live a life of "could have been." However, we have two kinds of wills: "image related" (our persona's will) and "authentic." Only when we get in touch with our real and authentic will, will we have a happy life.

HOW DO WE TELL THOSE WILLS APART?

How do we separate our authentic wills from the external, image-related ones that we have incorporated into our personality for all kinds of reasons? When we realize one "image related will," something that comes from the head and not from the heart (since this kind of will is also an engine and can move things forward) we feel emptiness, unease. Something is missing and the feeling we experience is: "What? That's it?" Because those realized wills are not a part of our essence and therefore don't satisfy us. This, by the way, is the cause for the "we-have-it-all-and-still-are-not-happy" syndrome. We all know people who suffer from it.

On the other hand, "authentic will" is independent; it's our own, uninfluenced by criticism, hardship or unreasonableness. We have a complete emotional coverage for it and it is an independent entity—with no shame or apologies—unrelated to nothing or anything. Because true will, like a true prayer, is an absolute, quiet little knowledge (very little, by the way) that the thing we want is going to happen. And then it just happens. It's a very distinct zone in our soul. If you have ever been to that zone, even regarding the smallest thing, you know the feeling.

HOW ARE WE GOING TO MANUFACTURE ACHIEVEMENTS?

First, we write on a piece of paper everything that we have on our "to do" list that we keep putting off for later. We slice those tasks like salami, into small, thin slices and there you go, one little slice a day, no more! And before you know it, the list, just like the long lines in Disneyland, is done, thanks to being organized.

People warn us about that "exaggerated will," that is like a landmine for achievement. But if it's exaggerated, it's not a will; it's an obsession and a compulsion. Hard-lining a certain desire or over-rating it will torpedo our achievements. And from the opposite angle: lightness—mind you, not lightness of the mind, but a light attitude (once again: a light attitude)—is what produces achievements. Only when we are connected to our authentic will that comes from our heart and our emotions, can we realize it easily thanks to a very strong tailwind. Our lives suddenly feel "at home." We have a sense of satisfaction and joy. The connection to our authentic will can attract solutions (strategies) to us like a magnet, it will become the engine that transforms fantasy into a reality. When a true will (gut feeling, intuition) meets our head (that provides the tactical-intuitive knowledge for how to accomplish what we want) we become laser-guided missiles and therefore, get to our target easily. The key word, as I said, is "easily" (in a subjective manner of course, because on the outside it sometimes seems unbelievably complicated). When we're there, we are unbeatable and we create our own miracles against all odds.

WANTING AND EATING

One of the main reasons that people become overweight is their personal desire, which is constantly suppressed. It is a classical conditioning that comes with a "cue" that we carry with us from childhood. This, by the way, is why people gain weight after the wedding, when the mutual "will suppression" begins. Just like you would give your seat in the bus to the elderly, their will relinquishes its seat for the will of loved ones. So where does their desire express itself, free of fear? In their plate of course! "I want food? Boom! Food happens for me right away!" Love handles also happen, but that is a small price to pay for not living a life of unsatisfied desires. What is the cure, you ask? That would be becoming the Hardy Boys of our wills: to become very aware of them, and to fulfill them with self-reporting and no guilt, because guilt abolishes self-giving. You chose to fulfill your will instead of the other and felt guilty about it? You annulled that self-giving. You ate and now you feel guilty? All the calories have attacked you and you are still left hungry and unsatisfied. All the dieters among you: attention!

I'm grateful to **Odetta** for giving me permission to publish her words, as well as for her support, encouragement and good advice along the way. Her words have certainly introduced new approaches to me, and were a guiding lighthouse for my now universal journey.

13 | OTHER GIFTS I HAVE RECEIVED THANKS TO THE LIST

As the days passed, the number of blog visits increased. Every day someone else discovered it and shared it with more people. Within weeks, the web counter showed thousands of visits a day and I had many offers of help.

Alon Gal, the leading life coach in Israel, the host of a prime time TV coaching show, and the owner of a reputable school for coaches, read one of my posts and contacted me:

"I have about a hundred coaches who are about to finish their semester in my school. I would love it if you came to tell them your story and what led you to *The List* and to self-fulfillment. Do you have a lecture about it?

I didn't. But two hours later, I did.

The lecture to his students was a success and I recounted it in detail in my blog and on my Facebook page. I must admit I was really excited about it. After all, who was I to present a lecture to 100 well-educated future life coaches?

Someone who had read about the lecture approached me to ask, "How much would it cost to book you for a lecture about achieving dreams as a part of a seminar for the Open University staff members?"

Me? Lecturing to the staff of an academic institution about achieving dreams? And getting paid for it? Please, someone pinch me so that I'll know it's not a dream!

Starting with dipping my toes into Alon Gal's wading pool ended with me falling headlong into an Olympic swimming pool. From the moment the rumor about my lecture began to spread, I started receiving invitations from leading companies—mobile phone companies, the national railway company, big banks, hotels, private gatherings, and more. I even starred as a "list stripper" in a very original bachelorette party. In just a few months, I had increased my annual income by more than thirty percent! I didn't see it coming. Not even in my wildest fantasies. I was just playing an Internet game with myself.

THE LIST STARTED WORKING FOR ME IN WAYS I COULD NEVER HAVE IMAGINED!

After publishing the blog, a computer technician offered me these sage words of advice: "Place advertisements in your blog. If you have a lot of traffic it may produce a few dollars a month. Every time someone clicks on an advertisement you'll get a few cents."

Three months later, I deposited a check for $102 from Google. Those were the happiest dollars I have ever earned. I hadn't done anything except express some thoughts on my blog and I received a nice little allowance. I continued getting more checks and then it hit me: I was going to use this money to fund my trip to Australia! All of a sudden, meeting a kangaroo in its natural habitat seemed closer than ever.

I also sent emails to Australian media agencies, to people in the Ministry of Foreign Affairs, and to the Ministry of Tourism in the hopes of attracting some media interest in my story and perhaps receiving a sponsored invitation covering my accommodation. I bombarded people with enthusiastic emails about my aquatic dream of surfing the waves of the famous Bondi beach. Most of the Australian officials I contacted never bothered to answer. I then realized that despite the flood of presents I had received, the road wasn't always going to be easy.

I can now see that my emails were not focused enough. They were mostly enthusiastic, funny, inarticulate, or simply too long. I didn't even bother to specify what they would gain from helping me. I could have pointed out the marketing opportunities that my visit, as the owner of a popular blog, could have opened up. I could have spoken about how people might decide to visit Australia after reading about it on my blog.

Over time I found out that every person who had volunteered to help me achieve any item on my list had done it for one of two main reasons; either out of sheer kindness, or because they were hoping to get exposure via the blog.

The moment I realized my mistake, I made sure I outlined the benefits that people would receive from helping me on my journey.

Nutritionists, trainers, coaches, psychologists, and even one psychiatrist contacted me after noticing the buzz the blog had generated. These people understood that by helping me they could gain online exposure, which in turn could translate to business expansion. From my perspective it was a fair enough barter; provide services and get exposure in return. It was a win-win deal.

14 | DANCING ALL THE WAY
TO THE BLOG

In my lectures there are always one or two people staring at me with this expression of: "Come on, everything that has happened to you happened because your name is **Yuval Abramovitz** and because you are famous and well-connected."

I assume that the same thought also crossed your mind when reading about the "miracles" that have happened to me and the famous people who have contacted me regarding my list. You may have a fair point. While it's true that in Israel my name means something to people, I am completely anonymous in other parts of the world where people may be unfamiliar with my work. To the people who have contacted me from Australia, USA, Japan, Norway, and even Iran, I'm just another anonymous resident of this planet.

Everything I have just told you about my personal journey up until this point is just an entrée to the endless feast that continues to this very day. It is now three and a half years since first publishing *The List* blog and not a day goes by without receiving at least one email related to *The List*. Support emails, personal exchanges, business offers, list suggestions, or new ideas to think about. I receive responses to my dreams as well as keys that may open the relevant doors. I like to think that I have established thousands of "embassies" around the world, each waving *The List* as its flag.

YOU CAN ALSO ESTABLISH "EMBASSIES" FOR YOURSELF AND FIND PEOPLE WHO WILL HELP YOU REALIZE YOUR DREAMS.

Why did all these people to take an interest in an anonymous guy and his peculiar list? In my opinion, it was the fact that I had overcome the classical conditioning (a result of our upbringing) that dictates we try and manage on our own, not to burden others who most likely have their own problems. I truly believe that it was the fact that I had dared to shout my dreams out aloud and ask for help.

I dared to stand up and announce: "Dear people, I need you. I need you to be a part of my journey toward the peak of my dreams because I will never succeed on my own."

Most of us were raised to not burden others with our problems and we try to behave accordingly and internalize that message. I think that it's working against us. Shame.

? | EXERCISE

Try to think: What is your biggest and wildest dream (doesn't matter how removed it is from reality), which might come true through an educated, careful use of social networks?

Can you imagine yourself broadcasting your dreams through the social networks? Whispering them to your closest friends? Sharing them with your colleagues?

If not, why not? What is keeping you from revealing your dreams to others? If you are not afraid to go public, what are you waiting for?

HURRY UP AND WRITE A STATUS ABOUT YOUR DREAM, OR TWEET IT!

15 | THE WORLD IS WRITING
LISTS

While the popularity of my blog was taking off, the most amazingly powerful and exciting thing happened, far more exciting than anything that's happened to me on my newly discovered yellow brick road. And like Dorothy, who was the greatest of dreamers, I have also been accused on more than one occasion of being somewhat delirious. My inbox filled up with private lists that people had sent from all around the world. People were connecting with the idea of vocalizing their dreams and asking to share their private dreams with me.

I received dozens of lists from Australia, Netherlands, Britain, China, Norway, Rwanda, the Palestinian Authority, United States, South Africa, Russia, Jordan, Iraq, France, Brazil, and more.

People wrote, shared, and in many cases asked for my opinion on their dreams. It filled me with pride and embarrassed me at the same time. Who was I to rate other people's dreams? Was I a "list master"? Did I have a "Notebook Scribbling List Expert" diploma? Back then the whole list idea was still new to me too, and also completely intuitive. When I first published the blog I didn't know that I was beginning my journey toward writing an effective list that could make dreams come true.

Despite the awkwardness of receiving these sometimes intimate lists from people I had never met and will probably never meet, and the fear of being nosy, I devoured them. These people embraced my little philosophy and helped me understand how much we are all alike. Just like the lyrics of **Jimmy Cliff**'s song "We all are one, we are the same person, I'll be you, you'll be me."

Many of those who have read the blog, both private and public figures, embraced the idea and started writing their own lists.

Take **Ido Tadmor,** for example, an international dancer and choreographer who published a list of dreams that included: Go on a world tour. Star in a musical. Produce a big show with dancers, actors, singers, and artists from other disciplines. Dance with **Baryshnikov.**

To this day Tadmor has yet to perform pirouettes with his idol, but he has already taken a few steps toward realizing this dream. Not long ago, he became the first Israeli to dance with the **Bolshoi Ballet**, the company who first featured Baryshnikov as a young dancer.

Tadmor also co-created a show with **HaYehudim,** one of Israel's most esteemed local rock bands, and checked "Produce a big show with artists from other disciplines" off his list. He has also traveled across Southeast Asia performing in a musical theatre piece.

Israeli singer **Ohad Hitman** is another artist who was inspired by the blog to publish his own list of dreams, including the following: Finish the play I have been working on for two years. Marry my boyfriend. Save money for the child we hope to bring into the world. Perform at the UN with a Mediterranean ensemble consisting of Israeli and Palestinian musicians.

Hitman published his list in May 2011. Three years later, his musical *Billy Schwartz* won first prize in The Festival of Musicals, where new musicals get first exposure. The prize money was ILS100,000 (about US$25,000). He married his boyfriend Ran in New York before returning to Israel and celebrating their marriage in a huge party. They are now going through the process of bringing a child into the world. Oh, and of course, Hitman performed with the Mediterranean ensemble in front of the European parliament. True, it's not the UN, but hey, this singer's dreams have materialized almost exactly as he had written them in his list.

There were hundreds of other dreamers from around the world who have asked to realize the dreams on their lists. Take Felicity from Australia, for example. She was the first Australian to offer me hospitality through Facebook, and the list that she posted on the blog was extremely moving. Here are some of her items: Organize a walking group of at least three people in my neighborhood. Grow fruit and vegetables. Complete at least forty more weeks of Hepatitis C treatments. Take the kids to the ocean. Abstain from sex, drugs, alcohol, and cigarettes due to the medical treatment I'm receiving. And take the risk of my family's rejection and make one last attempt to reconcile with them.

For a while there she updated me on the progress of her list. Among other things, she shared her emotional family reunion with me, told me about the new love she had found, and about the significant improvement of her health.

The List works for everybody. Famous or not. It's not the name that opens people's hearts, but a person's simple, straightforward request for help, whoever they may be.

"LONELINESS DOES NOT COME FROM HAVING NO PEOPLE ABOUT ONE, BUT FROM BEING UNABLE TO COMMUNICATE THE THINGS THAT SEEM IMPORTANT TO ONESELF, OR FROM HOLDING CERTAIN VIEWS WHICH OTHERS FIND INADMISSIBLE."

CARL GUSTAV JUNG

I could continue sharing page upon page and hundreds of dreamers' journeys; people who have dared to challenge their fear of publicly announcing their inner thoughts and succeeded.

Maybe some of those dreams were small, but not achieving them could be agonizing: A fifty-year-old who replaced his rotten teeth with a set of new dentures; a woman who lost about fifty-five pounds; a guy who sat himself down to write a book and finished it; someone who overcame her fear of water and started swimming; and some who found love.

Do you also want your dreams to come true? I'm confident that each and every one of the people who have had their dreams come true have not done it on their own. They were smart enough to connect the close, distant, and even virtual circles in their lives. Through the lists that were sent to me, I have discovered all of us have so much in common regardless of our age, gender, religion, financial background, social standing, or sexual orientation.

Believe it or not, we all share the same dreams: We all want to be skinnier and more fit (an item common to almost all the lists I have come across), we all want to take a long trip around the world or move to a foreign country for a while, a lot of us dream about publishing a book about our life story or writing the story that we always wanted to write.

Some of us are convinced that the invention we never told anyone about is going to change the world (when we have time and money to develop it of course!). Almost all of us dream about meeting famous people or our personal heroes. We want a big love to come into our lives and be a supportive life partner in return.

I sat down and prepared a summary of the lists I had received. I was curious to know what people's three most common dreams were.

These three dreams people shared time and time again were: Finding love, living in a bigger house, and being skinnier. However, every once in a while, I came across a list that contained more unique items. For example, one girl decided to establish a compound for abandoned dogs and asked for advice on how to start raising the funds for it. Another asked how to produce a gala evening to raise money for animals and animal rights. Someone wanted to skydive, bungee jump, or take on another extreme challenge. Someone wanted to go on a trip with their grandmother to discover their roots; others dreamed of developing a format for a reality show, anchoring a radio show, establishing a shelter for battered women, opening a vegan gourmet restaurant, taking care of an elderly person, and producing a Broadway show. A seventeen-year-old had a dream of being a screenwriter for Disney, and another wanted to open a vegetarian food center. And it went on and on.

16 DREAMS
IN MOTION

When I had over 200 lists waiting for me to read in my inbox, I decided to open a section in the blog called "Your Lists."

Anyone who had sent me a private list was invited to upload it to the blog along with their picture and contact details so that the world could respond to their list, just like it did to mine, and help materialize their dreams.

I emailed back to them: "Wonderful things happened to me and the same can happen to you too. I have no doubt that people will gladly help you too, and you can take advantage of the masses of people who visit my blog," and eagerly waited for people to post their lists on the website.

But most of the people who sent me private lists didn't upload them publicly on the blog.

As I mulled it over in my head, I couldn't understand the reasons for refusing to publish their lists to the blog and share their dreams with the world. I started a long, honest dialogue with each and every one of them asking them to explain what was preventing them from publishing their private list on my blog.

Based on the different answers I received, I suggest you check in to see how you feel about publishing your dreams. Do you refrain from sharing them? If so, do you know why?

? | EXERCISE

?   Where do you stand in regards to sharing your dreams? Can you easily do it, or do you dread the thought?

?   If I offered you the chance to publish your dreams on a popular website, or ask you to stand in front of a crowd of hundreds of people and announce your most desired dream in the hope that there is someone in the crowd who can help you realize it, would you do it?

If not, please write why. If it's the fear of exposure that is stopping you, is there a way to overcome that fear?

IF YOU ANSWERED YES TO THOSE QUESTIONS, YOU ARE ALREADY ON THE RIGHT TRACK TOWARD SENDING YOUR DREAMS OUT THERE.

IF YOU HESITATED IN YOUR ANSWER, I PROMISE TO PROVIDE YOU WITH A SAFETY NET THAT WILL HELP YOU DO THAT.

17 | WHY STIFLE OUR DREAMS AND NOT SHOUT THEM OUT?

I took the responses I received to the email I had sent out and put together a list of common reasons people gave for their reluctance to publish their list publicly:

✔ **I prefer to keep my dreams to myself**

✔ **I have no interest in letting people know what my future plans are**

✔ **I'm embarrassed**

✔ **It's too personal**

✔ **When I share my dreams, their energy dissipates.**

✔ **You only have dreams when you sleep; you can realize wills and desires, not dreams.**

On and on it went, reasons on top of reasons. The blog's "Your Lists" zone remained practically empty.

SO WHAT ON EARTH IS STOPPING US FROM SHOUTING OUT OUR DREAMS FROM THE ROOFTOPS? WHAT IS THE SOURCE OF THAT COLLECTIVE INHIBITION THAT CAUSES US ALL TO STIFLE OUR DESIRES AND KEEP THEM WELL HIDDEN?

Eventually I found a partial answer in the work of **Alfred Adler**, an Austrian doctor and psychotherapist.

The essence of Adler's work determined that the high level of cooperation and social culture (*Gemeinschaftsgefühl*) needed for one's existence in the world demands a spontaneous social effort—and education's main role is to stimulate that effort. Social feelings are not innate; their potential is innate and needs to be consciously nurtured. Adler also said "progress will never happen without awareness of what's preventing it from happening."

Thanks to Adler I finally understood that cooperation is a vital means to our existence, but also requires our efforts to achieve it (like continuing to go to the gym). I also learned that everything begins and ends with education, or more accurately, the kind of education we get at home. For many of us, though, our home education suppresses our natural spontaneity and damages our social effort's potential.

It's an education that warns us from coming across as arrogant, conceited, hedonistic, or greedy. It's an education that guides us, probably against our nature, to keep our dreams to ourselves and never share them with others.

I also discovered that keeping our dreams hidden sometimes has religious sources or is derived from superstitions that are passed on from one generation to the next.

People gave me highly intelligent explanations about the importance of modesty, of concealing personal weaknesses and of refraining from sharing problems with others. However, through conversing with these people, I realized that all this self-convincing is strongly affected by the most notorious dictator of them all: What will people say? What will the neighbors think? What will my friends say, or my teachers, or other dreamers? Dreamers who are actually sitting tightly on top of their own stack of dreams, worrying about preventing it from spilling over and revealing our selves.

Here is a letter I received from a fellow dreamer:

> "I'm enclosing my list but it is NOT to be published! I repeat: for your eyes only! I have thought about your charming project and your extensive work and tried to understand why it is so hard for me to publish my list. After all, I write columns in newspapers and on the Internet and I publish private things on Facebook, so what's the big deal? The answer I have so far come up with is that this is what I have been taught. It is not polite and not modest to dream of so much and—all the more—talk about it to friends. I was raised not to bother others with my private business and questions, and this is why I don't burden you with the things I'm curious about regarding your list. It's a kind of WASP etiquette."

Great. Not quite the chicken-and-the-egg causality dilemma, but the WASP-I-don't-want-to-bother-anybody-I'm-scared-I-forgot-how-to-be-me version.

This excuse has many forms and versions. A young girl who grew up in a religious house and who listened to my lecture quoted a Jewish source to me. According to that source: "There is no blessing but in the hidden from sight." When I scolded her and told her it was time to start shouting her hidden dreams, she stoically explained to me that one of the interpretations of this saying is that a man must not show off and boast about his achievements and successes and we must all be modest and humble. I truly respect others' beliefs, and consider myself a believer in my own way, and still I can't see how that girl's perception contradicts my absolute certainty, that in order to realize our dreams we have to shout them to the sky.

I have never encouraged anyone to publicly boast, nor have I had plans to take selfies of my new six-pack and upload it to the social networks. All I have ever asked was that we increase our ability to ask others for help up front, with no shame or blame.

THERE IS NOTHING CONDESCENDING ABOUT SHARING OUR DREAMS WITH OTHERS AND ASKING THEM TO HELP US REALIZE THEM. ON THE CONTRARY, TO ME IT SAYS THE EXACT OPPOSITE. I SEE IT AS MODESTY THAT COMES FROM A HIGH AWARENESS OF OUR LIMITED ABILITIES AS INDIVIDUALS, AS OPPOSED TO THE BIG AND EVER-INCREASING CAPABILITY THAT COMES FROM UNITING OUR POWER WITH THAT OF OTHERS.

MODEST DREAMERS

If some of you realize your wildest dreams but want to keep your successes to yourselves, so as not to rub it in people's faces, that is not a problem. Keep your achievements private. On the other hand, what about all the people who have helped you along the way? Don't they deserve to be happy for you? What about those who don't dare to try and realize their dreams? Don't they deserve to be inspired by your success?

That is one of the reasons you are now reading this book, one you found sitting alongside other books on the "inspirational, self-empowerment and guidance" shelf: to derive some courage from other people's heroic stories.

That is also why many of us read newspapers and magazines. In between the gossip pages and the recipes hide quite a few inspirational stories about people, both famous and unknown, who have overcome obstacles and reached the top, or were up to their noses in debt and managed to come out of their dire situation, or have faced a grave disaster and still keep a positive attitude toward life. I enjoy sharing my achievements with others, even though some (especially those who don't like me) may see it as boasting and self-aggrandizement. I just don't care. Let them have the wrong idea.

HAVE YOU EVER COME ACROSS A FLOWER THAT KEEPS ITS SEEDS INSTEAD OF SPREADING THEM AROUND, YET STILL DREAMS ABOUT THE NEXT SPRING?

18 | DREAM MUGGERS

Another thing I discovered was that many people don't share their dreams due to a fear that someone will steal their idea.

In one of my lectures, I met a woman with a college degree in interior design and dreams of opening her very own design store in her sleepy little village. She revealed to me her reasons why: "If I talk about my idea to open a unique design store in my village, I'm worried that someone will steal it." She has been fantasizing about opening that store since her first maternity leave and now has three children—how many years has she been carrying that dream around?

I answered: "Your village has existed for seventy years now, and no one else has opened a design store. Do you think that after seventy years, a one-eyed pirate is going to hear your idea and steal it just because he's overheard at the grocery store or read on Facebook that you have intellectual treasure buried somewhere? Are you really worried that posting one little status on Facebook asking for the help of experienced business people will inspire everyone to open a design store in your village? For seventy years, no one has opened any new stores, so why would they now? Remember, most people are busy with their own dreams and not with other people's."

"That's right!" jumped in a woman from the third row. "A lot of people imitate proven success instead of creating something new. Look how many bootlegs and copycats there are of iPhones, Crocs, and even frozen yogurt . . ."

In spite of my best efforts and attempts to convince her otherwise, I couldn't see this particular dreamer casting aside her fears to sign a business contract when she couldn't even bring herself to expose her dreams to the world and ask other people to help her with her idea.

Here's the scoop: We are all afraid to commit.

So the question is: "Why are we afraid of sharing our dreams with others?" Among the multiple explanations I received for that question, there was one particularly stubborn reason that turned up in almost every lecture:

"PUBLISHING A LIST OF GOALS IS A COMMITMENT."

It was another breakthrough: We are afraid to commit, even to ourselves, but especially in front of other people.

Let's go back to our friend Adler, who said:

 ## "THERE CAN ONLY BE ONE OBJECTIVE TO EDUCATION, AND IT IS EDUCATION TO COURAGE."

Fear, as I quickly discovered, is the most paralyzing thing that can happen to us on our journey to self-fulfillment. Fear is not just the opposite of bravery; it's the opposite of love. How do I know? Because the moment we stop fearing somebody or something, we can start to love it.

No one is immune to fear.

I experience fear, but I do my best to chase away those paralyzing thoughts. People sometimes question my hectic way of life, which must at times seems intense. I explain to them that the only reason I am traveling so fast is that if I slow down, I will have time to think about the bumps in the road.

Every time I put up a new post on my blog or a new status on my Facebook page, I write the post, launch it, and move on. I don't stop to think over what I have just done, or how embarrassing it may or may not be. Yes, sometimes it is a little dangerous, but if you don't try then you will never succeed. People have said all sorts of things about me, that I have a "brave character" or that I "don't care about anything," both of which are excuses for the fear they feel when considering a similar action and for why they struggle to succeed in achieving their dreams.

I am the first to admit that I can be a coward, yet at some point over the years I decided that I wouldn't let my fears control me. My public successes and public failures, my joys and disappointments have drawn both praise and criticism over the years and have helped me to develop a shield against the extreme remarks, and to accept and use the best advice, negative and positive, to my advantage.

ONCE WE STOP FEARING SOMETHING OR SOMEONE, WE BECOME CAPABLE OF LOVING.

19 | BETWEEN FEAR AND IMPULSE
BETWEEN REALIZATION AND CESSATION

For many years I have been claiming that the most fatal disease is not cancer or AIDS, but fear. Fear is the thing that makes us die while we are still alive. A dear friend once reminded me of **Julius Caesar**'s sentiments:

"A BRAVE MAN DIES ONCE. A COWARD DIES EVERY DAY OVER AND OVER AGAIN."

Fear has a greater control over us than love and stifles the will to realize our aspirations. People are afraid to take steps, whether big or small, that will take them out of their comfort zone. They are afraid of changes that will force them to recalculate their route, and maybe even compel them to reinvent themselves. They hold on to the familiar, even after it has been emptied of meaning and has become an empty shell. Even though that place is no longer good for them, they refuse to uproot. Like a plant whose roots are breaking out of the planter and whose stem is scraping the ceiling, but it still insists on clinging to its old pot. God forbid they should move away from the familiar place, or lose their grip. And so they twine, twist, bend, and groan silently. Slowly, without even realizing it, they wither.

People prefer the narrow worldview of their known limitations; they cling to it even though it causes discomfort and pain. The unknown remains the dreaded "other," even if it clearly entails hope and change for the better.

Too many single people are afraid to expose their love for another man or woman, preferring to act indifferently so as not to disclose their feelings. Too many couples are afraid to break up long after the relationship has lost its magic. They are afraid of losing their part of the common property, damaging their reputation or endangering the future of their children. Others are afraid to move, afraid to leave a job, afraid to end an unhealthy friendship, even afraid to change the color of their living room wall. If it sort of works, why change it? Why rock the boat?

It might be functioning but is it exciting and stimulating too? Is it alive?

We sacrifice our tomorrow on the altar of the fear that is in control of our lives today. We sacrifice our chance for change on the altar of neglect and convenience and let greyish shades color our lives. Then we display that cowardly behavior to our children, who learn to perpetuate and reproduce the same destructive code that is killing our own dreams because, if we go back to Adler for a second, education is first and foremost by personal example. Our children are educated not through what we tell them to do or not to do, but through assimilating our own behavior. No words needed.

OUR OWN FEAR IS KILLING OUR CHILDREN'S DREAMS AS WELL.

☑

A few weeks ago, I was wandering the streets of Tel Aviv with my five-year-old, Shira. It was dusk and all of a sudden Shira stopped, looked up to the sky, closed her eyes, and mumbled something.

"What happened?" I leaned over.

"I saw a shooting star so I made a wish," she whispered in my ear.

"What did you ask for?" I was curious.

"I can't tell you," she said, frowning at me. "If I tell you it will never come true."

We kept walking, hand in hand. I smiled at my little girl but I couldn't help but think about *The List* effect that has worked so well for me. How was I going to let her keep her wishes deep inside? I stopped and told her:

"Shira, I think you are wrong. I believe that if you choose to tell me your wish there is a bigger chance it will come true because maybe I can help you realize it."

She looked at me suspiciously.

"Take for example, when I was about your age, I went with Grandma and Grandpa to the Western Wall in Jerusalem. I wrote my wish on a note for God and put it in between the big stones. My wish came true; I got a computer, just like I had wished for!"

"God read your note?" Shira opened her big, blue eyes wide.

"I'm not sure about that"—I smiled and winked at her—"but I'm pretty sure that Grandpa had picked up the note and told Grandma and she got me the computer."

Shira didn't need more than thirty seconds to process the new information and immediately decided to share her wish with me.

"I asked for our family to be healthy," said my little humble girl.

I happily concurred with her wish.

What do we actually know about pursuing our dreams and wishes? What have our parents, their parents, and their parents' parents taught us? That if we see a falling star, we should make a silent wish. That if one of our eyelashes falls out, we should make a silent wish. Even on our birthday, *the* happiest day of our life, we blow out candles and make a silent wish.

Why should our wish remain in our hearts? After all, who hears it? Why not express our heartfelt wishes and dreams out loud? Why not say to our friends and family who have gathered to celebrate our birthday: "Hi, dear friends and family! How great it is to see you all here! You know what I'm dreaming of this year? To fly to Brazil and dance in the Carnival—until I drop from exhaustion. But guess what? I'm not able to pay for the trip. So maybe instead of buying me a shirt that I don't need or a book I'm not interested in, simply put twenty dollars in this box. That would help me pay for my dream's fulfillment. Thank you!" Why not help others fulfill our dreams?

The sweet birthday tradition, of blowing out the candles on a cake and making a secret wish, is appropriate in the world of little kids, where fairies fly, unicorns can talk, and Disney princesses ride in a carriage toward the sunset.

THE PROBLEM BEGINS WHEN TOO MANY PEOPLE ADOPT THAT TRADITION AND CONTINUE IT INTO THEIR ADULT YEARS—AND NOT ONLY ON THEIR BIRTHDAY. MANY CONTINUE TO HIDE THEIR WISHES BEHIND SUPERSTITIONS. THAT TRADITION CONTINUES AND IS PASSED ON FROM ONE GENERATION TO ANOTHER. TEACH YOUR CHILDERN AND THE PEOPLE AROUND YOU TO SHARE THEIR WISHES AND TO TALK ABOUT THEM.

20 | JUST LIKE REVEALING A WELL-KNOWN SECRET

I have a close friend who is charming, talented, energetic, and beautiful, with a great sense of humor. She is nearing forty and doesn't have a life partner. One evening, we were having a glass of wine together when she confided in me:

"I work all day with children and don't get to meet men my age. I don't connect to the whole Internet dating scene and I feel stuck in the single zone," she said.

"I have an idea," I said. "As someone who has known you for almost twenty years, I'm going to put a picture of you up on my Facebook page and share with people some of your brilliant qualities. People will get to know you and your dream of finding a good man to share your life with and this way we're bound to receive a few appeals from brave, open men who will be glad to accept the challenge."

Her appalled look said it all.

"Have you lost your mind? Let everybody know I'm lonely?"

"You're not lonely, you're looking for love," I replied. "Just like all the other people in the world. What's your problem with declaring it out aloud?"

"Because people will think I'm a failure when it comes to relationships."

There. This is how our fears take control of our logic. After all, we all know she is single, and at her age, even she considered herself to be "a relationship failure." It's a well-known secret. So why not express it in order to try and change the situation?

So what happened with my beautiful talented friend? By the end of the evening and the bottle of wine, we compromised. I wasn't going to share her wish with my friends, but she agreed to send an email to 100 of her friends, letting them know she was looking for a match. We agreed that this way she would get at least some suggestions in the right direction and indeed she did. She went on four dates, one of which led to a relationship that lasted a month.

As I'm writing these lines, she is still single, but I have not given up on her. So if you are reading this book and smiling because you think you can be the other half of such a great (though a tad picky) woman, please write to me through my website (the address is at the end of this book) and I will gladly connect you with each other. I also volunteer to conduct your wedding ceremony.

But I do understand the fear of my good friend whom I dearly love, for even though I speak highly of bravery and publicity, I feel it too. I recognize it—I acknowledge it. Then I figure out the best way to tackle it.

When *The List* became a lecture, I started receiving invitations to perform it for audiences around the world. When the news about writing this book leaked to the media, I received phone calls and offers for meetings abroad. I was ecstatic about the wealth that was being laid at my door, but at the same time, I started to get nervous. Now that my life seemed well sorted out, with a successful business, a steady career, a daily afternoon nap, and two daughters, this appeared to be an unwanted diversion. I was going to have to sell part of my business that required close management, be absent and be away from my home and family. Talking things through with close friends and relatives reassured me that every situation has a solution, especially one with this many positives. Speaking up about my fears led to a whole boxful of creative solutions and help, handed to me by those who wanted to see me succeed.

21 | THE BOLD
AND THE WRITING

My charming friend isn't the only person who came around to the idea of sharing her dream with others. A group of list writers uploaded their lists to my blog and within a short period of time, *The List* effect started to work for them as well.

People began sending me daily updates of how much weight they had lost (in my opinion, *The List* is responsible for wiping at least fifty tons of human fat from the face of the Earth so far). They documented adored family recipes for safekeeping, and captured on video the treasured stories of their parents and grandparents (most of us want to do it but don't find the time until it's too late).

The brave people who have uploaded their personal lists tell stories of strangers contacting them after reading their lists online and offering to help them.

Take for example the keychain factory owner who contacted another fellow list writer who wanted to raise money for animals in need. He donated outdated stock to her so she could sell it for a low price and use the money to realize her dream.

One dreamer had fantasized for years about meeting the band **Roxette** and when he finally did, it was thanks to other Internet users who helped.

A strange woman stopped me in the street to tell me that the baby in her baby carrier was adopted. She decided to adopt a baby thanks to *The List* blog.

In return I also did my best to help list writers take a step or two toward realizing their dreams.

I suggested to an Israeli reporter who had moved to Berlin, and encountered difficulty in finding work as a writer, to write her articles in Hebrew, have them translated to German, and offer them to the German newspapers. "While a big part of your income will go straight to the translator, you will get your foot in the door while learning the language and the field." Two weeks after accepting my advice she got a job with a reputable Berlin local newspaper.

A young man, who suffers from ALS, wrote in his list that he wanted to publish a column that would expose his battle with the disease and chart his progress in order to inspire others. He thought that whatever he could do, anybody could. I recommended he send his story to some websites and soon after, his first inspiring and stimulating column was published on one of the leading online news sites in Israel.

A thirty-three-year-old woman shared with me her dream to become an actress: "I know it will never happen," she wrote at the end of her list. I sent her a list of Israeli and international actresses who have become famous at a mature age after having dared to listen to their hearts. The dramatic dreamer got the necessary courage, auditioned for a professional acting school, was accepted, and began her journey toward her dream.

FINALLY, THE LIST HAD STARTED WORKING FOR OTHERS TOO.

22 | THE SECRET OF
THE LIST

In response to *The List*, people say: "So, your list is actually like that book *The Secret*, right? Think positively and then things will come true for you?"

Like the many who find the idea behind *The Secret* enthralling, I connected immediately to the theory of positive thinking.

This is how I have always lived. If not for the positive thinking and optimistic attitude that I inherited from my mother and grandmother (and my first *The List* notebook), I would still be in a wheelchair to this day.

When in dire straits, it's very easy to sink into melancholy. Positive energy pulls us out of this trap.

As people talk to me about the similarities between *The List* and *The Secret*, a common theme for those seeking answers emerges.

Many of the people looking for paths to self-fulfillment depend on the types of positive thinking found in self-help books: Think positive and positive things will come to you. While this is a worthy attitude, it is also one that leaves you passive.

JUST THINKING?
WHAT ABOUT DOING?

Great, they wrote themselves an imaginary check for a million dollars, or cut a picture of their dream home out of a magazine and hung it on their refrigerator door, but they have not taken so much as one step other than wait for the positive thoughts they had sent toward their dream to make it come true.

One essential thing has been left out of this picture: In order for things to happen, imagination is not enough. Dreaming and acting must be conducted simultaneously:

DREAM—AND PERFORM.

I believe in positive thinking, but I know with great certainty that thoughts alone are not enough. It's not "the universe" that hears us, but people. That is why I aim my dreams at the eyes and ears of people who can help me.

THE ARGUMENT ABOUT THE EXISTENCE OF A SUPREME BEING IS AS OLD AS HUMANITY AND ALTHOUGH I CONSIDER MYSELF A MAN OF BELIEF, WHEN IT COMES TO MY OWN PRIVATE PRAYERS, I MAKE SURE TO LAUNCH THEM AT PEOPLE AROUND ME.

IT DOESN'T MATTER WHETHER YOU ARE CHRISTIAN, JEWISH, MUSLIM, HINDU, OR IF YOU BELONG TO ANY OTHER FAITH, FOR THAT MATTER. IT ALSO DOESN'T MATTER IF YOU BELIEVE IN THE EXISTENCE OF A GOD OR NOT. MY APPROACH IS RELEVANT FOR YOU TOO.

IT IS YOU I LAUNCH MY DREAMS AT, AND AT THE SAME TIME, I URGE YOU TO HELP OTHERS TOO.

23 | ABOUT DREAMERS AND START-UP ENTREPRENEURS

The people who most profoundly understood the principle of marketing your dreams are the big start-up entrepreneurs of the end of the twentieth century and beginning of the twenty-first century. We are talking about the visionary and highly motivated type of people who first dream and then execute.

They announce a new technological development, a new application, an electric car, or other invention. Then they knock on every investor's door out there, give interviews to the financial newspapers, and do whatever is in their power to create a buzz around their dream product while they are still working on its development and production.

I'M HAPPY TO SHARE A LITTLE TRICK I USE WHEN I START A PROJECT: I SHOUT IT OUT LONG BEFORE IT EVEN EXISTS.

"Shouting out" my project enables me to examine its business potential through the reactions of people.

For example: about three years ago I met my friend **Amnon Jackont,** an esteemed writer and editor, for lunch. Amnon became my close friend after having edited my second book. We have both been teaching writing in different institutions and at some point we were both tired of the settings in which we were teaching. I had an idea to open, for the first time in Israel, a school for writers of all genres, starting with status updates for social networks and blog posts through to writing song lyrics, screenwriting and theatre, and journalism and prose.

Even after nailing down the concept, we still weren't sure the idea would work. On one hand, we were trying to penetrate a very saturated market (there were many writing workshops in Israel), and on the other hand, we would be offering our students a unique tasting menu to pique their interests and develop their palates.

Since we didn't know how to reach our potential market, we decided to "shout out" our dream. We approached many renowned writers who we wanted to join our staff, and asked for their permission to use their names. Our next step was getting Internet advertising for a small amount (about $1500) and this is how we started "shouting" the existence of our school.

At that point, we didn't even have a venue for our school yet, not to mention students, but after two days of "Internet noise," our Facebook friends started to ask for details and two weeks later, we had enough students for the first class. Today, a year and a half later, we have 180 students in several classes that take place simultaneously.

☑

I used the same system to draw attention to my first novel, *Here Is Yael Weiss, Tel Aviv*. The plot of the book is about a young woman who moves from a small northern town to Tel Aviv, with the purpose of conquering the big city and becoming famous. She lands a job at a small, failing news channel where she exposes corruption behind the scenes of the media world, to the point of risking her life.

I thought long and hard about what was going to convince a person going into a bookstore to select my book from the shelf, out of the hundreds of other books that were going to be displayed in front of them, take it to the cash register, pay for it, and take the time to read it. It was clear to me that I had to "shout" the publishing of the book out in order for the book to make its way to the best-sellers list.

I went to a printing house and for about $150 I had 1000 stickers printed with "threatening" messages on them in the spirit of my mystery novel: "Yael Weiss, we know where you live." "Yael Weiss, we are going to get you." "Yael Weiss, you can't evade us forever."

I asked a few friends to help and we went out on a Friday night to spread the stickers all over Tel Aviv. In less than three hours a man came to us to ask who Yael Weiss was. We explained about the promotional technique and the curious man, who turned out to be a journalist, wrote about my original technique in his newspaper. Later, there were mentions on websites and thanks to the coverage, after two weeks, my book was rated ninth on the best-seller list.

IN A WORLD SO SATURATED WITH INFORMATION, WHERE ALMOST EVERY PERSON HAS SOMETHING TO OFFER OTHERS, WE HAVE NO CHOICE BUT TO SPEAK UP AND STAND OUT IN THE CROWD.

Many websites invite inventors and artists to share their dreams with the world and raise the money to realize their dreams using the support of the crowd. This is how I financed the original publication of the book you are now holding. I will elaborate more on that toward the end of this book and will give you some tips in case you want to do the same.

☑

Personal marketing via the new Internet world is an exercise in externalizing their dreams.

Barack Obama swept millions of people behind him during the course of one brilliant campaign that bypassed the mainstream, old-fashioned media channels and focused on the Internet. He and his staff successfully shouted out their dream of a change, the result of which was Obama's inauguration as the first African American president of the United States.

☑

Once, at the end of a lecture, a young man came to me and said that the idea of a list and its publicity was charming, but not for him.

"Lists are for people who stand out in the crowd, extroverts like you," he told me.

I looked at myself from top to bottom. Me? Standing out? I was wearing a simple pair of jeans, a cheap T-shirt, and a pretty regular pair of sneakers. The only thing that was different about me was my hairdo, which ends in a pointy tip. So I answered him: "I don't think I'm that much of an extrovert. That's a description that would fit someone like Lady Gaga, who goes around wearing colourful wigs and dresses made out of steaks. And you know what? Look how far she got thanks to her extrovert personality."

Stefani Germanotta, a dreamer from New York, became the billboard Top 100 singer that she is by creating a buzz to promote herself. She "shouts out" about her art in order to make it stand out above other singers in the world. We no longer live in a pre-cable TV world where an interview on a leading talk show can turn someone into a star overnight.

Stars like Lady Gaga understand that in order to be heard, they have to shout louder than ever before.

Yes, noise is sometimes a necessary tool for advertising yourself, and must be in the toolbox of someone who wants to break into a public consciousness that's already so saturated with stars, YouTube clips, reality TV shows, millions of websites, social networks, newspapers and TV channels. Life is hectic!

So it doesn't matter if you are fans of the lady, or if she gets on your nerves, you must agree that we are talking about a practical and talented woman. True, she has a good voice, an impressive ability with musical instruments, and she can certainly move, but mostly she has a staff of creative people who work for her and make sure she is noticed.

MAKING SURE YOUR IDEA/PRODUCT/VISION IS VISIBLE, RECOGNIZED, AND WELL-KNOWN DOES NOT MAKE YOU ARROGANT AND BOASTFUL; IT MAKES YOU AN EFFICIENT AND EFFECTIVE PERSON.

The young man who asked the question thought a bit, and eventually explained that he didn't mean to call me arrogant and boastful, but that being a journalist, an author, an actor, and an entrepreneur, I'm a public persona and as such, he said that it was clear that shouting my dreams and expressing them out loud would be easier for me.

I agreed with him and understood why publicity was hard for him. I had been trained to express my thoughts and opinions columns and in newspaper articles. But in the same breath, I suggested to him the same thing I had suggested to my single friend: "If you can't work up the courage to shout out loud, then whisper your dreams. But do it clearly and to at least 100 people who know you. If you don't know 100 people, then do it in your close circle of family and friends. Harness your world in your favor."

❓ | EXERCISE

❓ THINK ABOUT ONE OF YOUR DREAMS FOR A MOMENT.

Who are the people around you who would be happy to help you advance toward this dream if only they knew about it? Are there any people you can think of? Write them a graceful letter RIGHT NOW to tell them about your dream and about how you think they can help you to realize it.

People are already starting to understand the power of the crowd, and the importance of effective use of social networks. Telling other people about what you prepared for lunch, bickering about your daily tasks, and woohooing about the upcoming weekend may be nice, but is of no importance and significance.

A smart use of social networks is one that generates change, either for you or for others, a use that succeeds in changing reality and creating a better tomorrow. Make more efficient use of the Internet. Build the right crowd and when you decide it's the right moment to seriously move ahead, derive help and support from it.

Parade your dreams around on every possible platform and activate the world in your own favor. Make yourself a priority. Put thought and time into your different social network profiles.

For example, I regard my Facebook profile as a magazine that I own. I fondly call it "Yuval Times" and as of now, it has over 9,000 subscribers.

In my "newspaper" I write thoughts on life (editorials), upload selfies and relevant photographs (gossip column), share pictures of my family life (photos of children generate tons of "likes." In light of such success, I'm now considering adopting a dog), and start heated discussions about politics and matters of the day. I also have an entertainment section in which I entertain my readers, recommend restaurants and cultural events, and share my favorite songs and movies.

In return for the free reading material that I provide for my followers, I ask for their help in distributing my dreams from time to time by clicking the "Share" button. I once managed to make 1688 people share a very quarrelsome status that might have been hastily and sloppily written, but was also from my heart and nerves, against a coupon company that had avoided payment for six months. They owed me the money for a big deal I had made with them to sell coupons for one of my businesses. Lo and behold, forty-eight hours from the moment this status had spread wings, it got an exposure of about a million readers (!) and made its way to the headlines of the big financial newspapers. I was invited to their office to receive my money in cash, and in a lump sum. It wouldn't have happened without the support of my readers.

That was the point when I understood how quickly my status as a public figure had gone viral. It was a defining moment for me (much like when I had located John Amaechi so surprisingly easily) that helped me thoroughly understand the possibilities lying at the tips of my fingers on the Internet and the mighty force of social networks.

More than once I have encountered human stories that go viral on the web. Like the story of a man who had passed the age of forty and was having a hard time finding a job. Or the story of a private shop whose owners were battling the chain stores and were asking for help. There are touching stories like that of twelve-year-old Louis Corbett from New Zealand who was told by his doctors that he was going to lose his eye sight to Retinitis Pigmentosa within a few months. Louis had composed a list, with some help from his parents, of things he wanted to see before he lost his vision. Among other things, his list included seeing some rare panoramic views and watching his favorite basketball team, the Boston Celtics, play. His parents opened a Facebook account for the purpose of raising the money to make their son's wishes come true. Within a short time, they raised $25,000 from strangers from all over the world who were touched by their son's story.

MAKE IT A HABIT TO SHARE A STATUS, ONCE A WEEK, IN WHICH YOU WILL ASK FOR SOME KIND OF HELP FROM YOUR FRIENDS, AND TOGETHER WE WILL CREATE A DREAMING, SHARING, HELPING, AND REALIZING WORLD OF PEOPLE. THANKS TO THE WONDERS OF TECHNOLOGY, THE POWER TO HELP OURSELVES AND EACH OTHER IS IN YOUR HANDS.

24 | WHAT IS IT GOOD FOR
ANYWAY?

My blog had only been online for two days when I started hearing from family and friends wondering: "What is this nonsense?"

Some of them warned me that I was already a busy person, managing a career and raising a family and that they felt it was stupid, public, and superficial to chase after dreams like six-packs, a trip to Australia, rehabilitating homeless people, or meeting Oprah.

"You spend too much time on your blog," commented a close friend.

"Just don't hurt your businesses and your livelihood," warned a relative.

"What's that list good for anyway?" wondered a colleague at the newspaper I work for.

Pretty quickly I found answers to all of these questions. Answers that came from the emails and lists I received and the conversations I was having on a daily basis. In the end, I responded to their questions with a question of my own:

WHAT ABOUT YOU? WHEN WAS THE LAST TIME YOU SIGNED A CONTRACT WITH YOURSELF?

25 | WHEN IT'S WRITTEN, IT HAPPENS!

We sign contracts throughout our lives: when we get married, get a divorce, buy a house, open a bank account, and start a new job. Even when we buy a cellphone for a few hundred dollars, we are actually signing a binding contract with the carrier.

Only with ourselves do we never sign any contracts. We are so preoccupied with our careers, raising children, caring for our relationships, and even just day-to-day survival, that we never find the time to commit to ourselves.

WAIT: DON'T SUCCEED . . . OR DON'T REALLY WANT TO?

With hand on heart: When was the last time, if ever, that you sat in front of a blank paper, wrote yourself (in hand writing!) a list of commitments, and told yourself that you commit to doing those things in the upcoming year? When did you ever commit to yourself that if you don't carry out those commitments you would fine yourself with a substantial penalty?

Your answer is probably "never." Best-case scenario, you are now mumbling, "I have a list like that in my head."

Why is it that when we go shopping we take the time to write a grocery list, but we never do it for our own lives?

Many times, people attending my lectures explain to me that they don't need a pen and paper to write a list, because the list is in their head, or somewhere on their smart phone (buried under dozens of reminders and hundreds of pictures). While that's nice, it's not enough, especially in the noisy era we live in, when we are available on the phone almost all the time, when more and more people are diagnosed with attention and focus disorders, and when the amount of information we are exposed to daily is huge. All of those distractions can easily blur the lists floating around our brain.

Speaking of penalties, there are ways to get technology to help us with that too. I've recently heard about applications and international websites, such as *stickK*, which encourage people to commit themselves to performing certain tasks. If you are committed, you entrust some money as collateral. The website's inspectors, along with a "supervisor" (a family member or a friend), follow your progress and if you don't perform what you have committed to, the money you entrusted is donated to charity.

A WRITTEN LIST AND THE CEREMONY OF WRITING IT, I'VE DISCOVERED, HAVE A FAR GREATER POWER THAN A LIST THAT WE KEEP IN OUR HEAD. A WRITTEN LIST IS THE MIRROR OF OUR HEART'S DESIRES AND A VISUAL REMINDER OF OUR WILLS. A DREAM IS JUST AN ABSTRACT THOUGHT OR A FANTASY UNTIL IT IS WRITTEN ON A PAPER AND BECOMES A COMMITTED GOAL!

So why are we so afraid of committing to ourselves? Why are we afraid that a written list, in black and white, will force us to come face to face with a commitment?

I noticed that many of those who sent me their lists hesitated to publish them out of fear that this would publicly commit them, but mostly it would commit them to themselves. We know that writing a list commits us to execute it, which is the very same thing that prevents us from committing in the first place. However, if our goal is to realize the dreams we articulate, what is wrong with something holding us to our commitment?

So here is my answer to the worried relative, the colleague who fears for the stability of my career, and the close friend who is jealous of the hours I spend on the blog:

When we run a list in an organized and an effective manner, we start to be attentive to, and aware of, our heart's desires and of where we want to arrive. The list is a map of the way and it shows us the right lane, much like Waze, one of the world's largest community-based traffic and navigation apps. It's a constant reminder of the final destination we aspire to reach in a certain time frame.

Written dreams are like a contract we have signed with ourselves. As soon as we write them and display them in a visible place, we become committed to them. On the other hand, when a list is wandering in our head with no focus, it gets lost. Like a horse with blinkers limiting its side view so that it doesn't stray from the designated route, we are walking in what we think is the main road, which is supposed to lead us safely to a fulfillment of our aspirations, but is actually a distraction, making us miss numerous other side roads that can lead us to the achievement of other goals. When our list is written, organized, and is with us throughout our day, we are much more attentive to and aware of what is happening around us. Without the blinkers, we become open, our senses sharpen and we recognize more and more opportunities that cross our way. All of a sudden, we overhear in the café a group of people at the next table incidentally talking about one of our dreams. All of a sudden it turns out the man next to us on the plane can connect us to someone who can significantly advance us toward one of our goals. This is how we open ourselves to opportunities, thanks to an accurate wording of our goals.

We can go to a friend's birthday party and be surrounded by many strangers and loud music, and still we'll overhear that guy who talks about his intention to open a restaurant and about how he needs a partner. That partner could be anybody in the crowd around him, standing with a drink in their hand, including you. This is how you start to recognize opportunities.

Does it remind you of something? Like getting pregnant and suddenly seeing a lot of pregnant women around you, or when you are a student and suddenly you start noticing a lot of other students in the street? And maybe when you are getting married and suddenly it seems like everyone is shopping for a wedding gown? We tend to recognize people who are in the same state of mind as us. Maybe it's our need for belonging. Abraham Maslow has mentioned it long before me, in his Hierarchy of Needs.

Even business people, corporate executives, and others who have already fulfilled themselves in the professional field (thanks to lists and periodic planning, by the way), need lists in their private lives. Those lists will help them improve their quality of life and help them manage what little free time they have to get the most out of it in terms of family relationships, friends, and personal goals, which are sometimes cast aside due to their demanding career.

I often lecture to senior businessmen, owners of $5 million businesses. I enjoy listening to their personal lists, which convey a desire and longing for more quality time with the family, and mostly some more pampering for their neglected spirit or body.

One very successful real estate businessman, who owns assets in Israel, London, and New York, told me in one of *The List* workshops that he had no more dreams, since he has already them all.

"A little sad, isn't it?" I deliberately taunted him. "What makes you want to get out of bed in the morning?"

He kept silent. Counting money or signing checks may be very boring and routine. At the end of the meeting he admitted that his life had indeed become routine, but on the other hand, he didn't see any need for lists and dreams since he already had plenty of money and he could realize everything without much thought.

"But what do you still want that you don't have?" I took interest.

"A wonderful woman to fill the emptiness that my wife's death has left seven years ago," he said with misty eyes.

"Well, write a list of steps to take that will help you find a companion for the second chapter of your life and start walking!"

He smiled and promised to try and commit to finally overcome the deep grief that had been a part of his life for so long and to start taking care of himself.

HOWEVER, A LIST IS NOT JUST A CONTRACT. A LIST IS ALSO PURE FUN. A PUBLIC LIST CAN PAINT YOUR LIFE IN PINK.

Regardless of our occupation, our lives eventually take up a routine track—predictable and somewhat gray. True, there are peaks, moments of transcendence, of breaking boundaries and barriers, but most of it is hard work and mundane tasks.

You may be surprised, but this is also how the biggest movie stars who frequently visit the shiniest parties in the Cannes and Berlin film festivals feel. How do I know, you may ask? I've met many of them. I have visited many of these parties myself, with the royalty of Dubai, Monaco's high society, and world celebrities. At the end of the day, they all want to get out of the corsets, the fancy dresses and rented tuxedoes, and change into comfortable sweat pants. And if even they are occasionally bored with their shiny lives, what are we—the ordinary people—supposed to feel?

THIS IS THE REASON WHY I'M SO CONSISTENT WITH MY METHOD OF WRITING LISTS. IT ENABLES ME TO MAKE LITTLE SKIPS OF HAPPINESS EVERY DAY AND, MOST OF THE TIME, FOR FREE. FOR ME, THAT'S A LOT.

26 | INSIGHTS ON WEALTH AND HAPPINESS

In May 2014, days before sending the first edition of this book to print, I traveled to the Cannes Film Festival in France. As I was standing in front of the port of Monaco, one of the world's richest countries, I had an epiphany.

The answer to the question I've been asking myself for a long time occurred to me. The question is: Why does everybody need a list?

But before I share my moment of epiphany with you, I want to tell you about a friend I met when I was twenty-seven. That year, just before my birthday in November, I decided to mark the occasion (for the first time in my life) with a big party for all my friends. I rented one of Tel Aviv's leading nightclubs and invited hundreds of friends and colleagues past and present.

About an hour before the party, a close friend called to ask if he could bring a couple of friends with him. Of course it was fine by me, it's a party! The more the merrier.

My friend arrived at the peak of the evening. His friends kept apologizing for not bringing me a gift. They promised to make it up to me the next day and asked for my phone number, although I repeatedly said there was no need for a gift.

The next day I got a call from them asking me what my plans were for the rest of the week.

"Work, get my head together after the party," I said. "Nothing special."

"Is your passport valid?" he asked.

I told him it was.

"Then we are going to fly together next Tuesday."

I thought he was joking, but agreed to his offer, completely bemused.

The day before the flight he rang me up again to make sure I was ready and gave me the lowdown of the trip. We were flying to London, in his private jet. This is how I first found out just how wealthy this stranger was who showed up uninvited to my party. As our friendship deepened I would eventually find out just how wealthy he really was. His daily interest equaled an average worker's monthly paycheck. Over time we grew closer and became very good friends. Our spontaneous visits to the world's capitals became a routine matter.

One day when I was in London for work, his name came up on my mobile phone.

"Where are you now?" he asked.

"Roaming Oxford Street," I answered.

"So take a cab and get yourself over to Soho. We're here to visit you."

We walked down the streets of the colorful neighborhood together, and I just couldn't contain my excitement for the city even though it was my tenth visit there.

"It's so great that we're here!" I said, "I love this town so much!"

"Sure," my friend replied rather indifferently.

"Aren't you happy to be here?" I tried to make sense of his lack of enthusiasm.

"I am, I am…" He trailed off unconvincingly. "It's just that I've been here so many times, it's not that exciting for me anymore."

From that moment on I couldn't help noticing the lack of enthusiasm that had taken over his life. It was very hard to excite or to move him. At thirty-seven, that young millionaire has seen and experienced it all (including a heart attack). The only thing he still found exciting was "conquering" new women that his fat wallet couldn't buy for him.

Back to my revelatory moment at the Cannes Film Festival.

Monaco is a small and extremely rich country, with zero unemployment rate, top designer shops, and a special police force (one policeman for every sixty citizens) to keep the peace. But at some point I realized I was roaming around this beautiful place, and nothing I saw excited me.

I thought the reason could be that I already knew much of the city, so I hired a private guide to show me around the Prince's Palace, the cheese market, the Cathedral, the port, and the marina. He took me to a spectacular vantage point from which I could see the French Riviera spread out like a post card. But still, it didn't move me.

For a moment there, I feared I had become like my rich friend. I'm no millionaire and I have not been around the world like he has, but I have seen quite a few markets, churches, palaces, mansions, and breathtaking natural wonders.

The guide went on and on about the wonders of Monaco, and the only thing I wanted to do was to try something new and different. Something I had never done before.

He spoke about Princess Grace, and all I could think about was knitting!

"I really want to learn to knit," I suddenly thought to myself. I have no idea where that peculiar idea came from, but what I did realize was that I needed to do things I had never done before and fly to places I had never been to.

I sat on a bench in front of the most breathtaking view in the world, pulled out my list notebook (which I always carry with me), and wrote the destinations of my next vacations: India, South Africa, and Antarctica. I remembered how excited I felt during my first trip to China, how it blew my mind to see people so different from me, a culture and a place so different from anything I had ever seen before.

I was again reminded of how important it is to list my dreams, as small as they may be. In fact it can and even should be composed of little, easy-to-realize, exciting, and refreshing items such as: Learn to sew. Read the Bible cover to cover. Paint the house. Grow plants in a flowerpot. Learn to cook gourmet meals. Tour a local city I have never visited before. Many more little things come to mind.

Paying attention to the little excitements that color our everyday lives is extremely satisfying and can add new sights, new sounds, and new smells to our daily routine.

I don't want to be numb or the kind of person who doesn't find excitement in the little things. The happiest people I've ever met lived in the Rio de Janeiro favelas. In those Brazilian slums, where most people live in tiny little apartments with many relatives and small children, I've met people who knew how to find joy in the smallest of things. I've met people who could surrender themselves to joyous music that comes out of a huge speaker in the neighborhood café, or just take pleasure in the spring weather.

Today I fear that our affluent culture is dulling our senses. I believe less is truly more and that too much of anything creates a certain deep sense of indifference in us.

ON THE BEACH OF MONACO, FACING ONE OF THE MOST BEAUTIFUL PANORAMIC VIEWS IN THE WORLD, I REALIZED I DIDN'T WANT TO LOSE THE ABILITY TO GET EXCITED, AND I UNDERSTOOD THAT THANKS TO MY LISTS, IT WILL NEVER HAPPEN.

27 | PUTTING OFF SELF-FULFILLMENT UNTIL
RETIREMENT

Like many before me, I have also found myself occasionally thinking "I'll get around to it when I retire."

I have a long list of books, plays, and films that I will read or watch one day when I have the time.

"Life is what happens to you when you're busy making other plans," sang **John Lennon**. I'm not sure that I'll ever have free time to get around to doing it all. I'm a frenetic entrepreneur—it's my nature—and I need to be constantly moving and doing something. When I do have free time, it is quickly gone, spent on hobbies, an afternoon nap, friends, and of course my family.

When I was younger, I convinced myself there was no need to rush and that everything could wait for my golden years. This is how I fell into the "one day when I have time" trap. But how do we know that we are going to get to our golden years? Two of my close friends have just recently lost their friend, a forty-three-year-old woman who went to sleep and never woke up.

While everybody who knew her was in complete shock and grief, I wondered whether or not her family had taken comfort in the fact that she fulfilled herself in her lifetime: She was a mother, had traveled the world, enjoyed professional success, and had many friends.

In the last two decades, young people of our generation have been crowned with many titles such as "generation X," "generation Y," the "selfie generation," and the "lost generation."

The fact that the world has become so accessible and presents infinite possibilities has caused many young people in the West to lose focus. We want it all, and we want it now. We dabble. As a self-proclaimed dabbler I see no problem with that. Doing promotes more doing and not just in one area of our lives. The problem starts when young people look ahead and think: "I still have a lot of time to make decisions regarding my 'real life'. There's time."

BUT THAT'S THE THING! REAL LIFE IS HERE AND NOW—AND LIFE BECOMES WHAT WE MAKE OF IT.

The decision to delay choices about the rest of our lives will only lead us to an endless search and a lack of focus. I know quite a few young people who started their professional lives later on, after having traveled in Southeast Asia or studied toward a degree, or hopped from one job to the other. When they come around they begin their professional life at the age of thirty on a minimum wage after having lost a whole decade. When they reach forty and are supposed to have some financial security, they're still supported by their parents and can't make ends meet.

I believe that listing and focusing should start at a young age.

PASS THIS MESSAGE ON TO YOUR CHILDREN.

28 | EXCUSE ME, KIDS, ## WHAT'S YOUR FOCUS?

Don't let your kids be a part of the lost generation. Teach them to focus on their goals and write their lists. Give little children and young adults credit for knowing and understanding (with the right guidance) the importance of focus in their lives.

When I present my lecture to teenagers I sometimes fear they will find it hard to connect to my message, to sympathize with it, or to understand it. But their openness surprises me every time. Young adults, who have yet to form incorrect ideas about what is possible and what is not, believe, very openly, that all doors are open for them and that all dreams can be realized.

Like **Peter Pan**, they still believe they can fly. I'm surprised every time by their maturity, their openness and their belief that the world is their oyster. Most of them have never suffered the blows that life deals us, and are yet to surrender themselves to the dictates of the adult world.

When I see a young couple holding hands I can't help but think about all the puppy love I missed because of the fear of being rejected. I was such an idiot for not asking girls on dates, simply because I was scared they wouldn't be interested in me.

A ten-year-old boy at one my lectures dreamed of meeting **Brian May**, the legendary Queen guitarist. He wrote it in his list of goals and decided that on Purim (the Jewish Halloween) he was going to dress as Freddie Mercury. His mother posted photos of him as Mercury on an international Facebook fan page and within a few minutes the pictures received more than a thousand "likes" and about fifty shares. As the numbers went up, they received many different suggestions about how to contact May directly. With so much originality, daring, and desire, I feel that it is only a matter of time until the boy and his mother will upload a picture of the much-desired meeting.

? | EXERCISE

? If you were told that within one year the planet Earth was going to be extinct, what are the ten things you would want to do in the time that you had left?

Quickly write down the first things that come into your head. Don't think too much.

IS THERE AT LEAST ONE THING ON YOUR LIST THAT YOU COULD START WORKING TOWARD TODAY? WHAT IS STOPPING YOU FROM DOING IT?

WHAT CAN YOU DO ABOUT IT? NOW. YES, RIGHT NOW! PUT THE BOOK DOWN, GET ON GOOGLE, AND TAKE THE FIRST STEP TOWARD YOUR DREAM.

"WHATEVER YOU LEARN IN YOUR YOUTH, YOU DO WELL IN YOUR OLD AGE."

(A DUTCH SAYING)

29 | BLACK GOLD

So many times people have said to me: "Where are you rushing to? Why burden yourself with the pressure? Do it when you retire!"

There is one problem with retirement, though: in many cases, the reality of the golden age is far from how we imagine it to be.

I am someone who has indirectly experienced the impacts of old age when I was forced to shuffle around slowly with a tennis ball–cushioned walker for a good stretch of time. There is no good reason to wait for your golden years to start your life. True, it may be a beautiful time in your life, but it may just as well turn out a lot less pretty than how you might picture it.

In my life I have had the honor of watching quite a few people grow old. Some have aged in a dignified, even enviable way, but the lives of others have slowly become empty and heartbreakingly sad. Having to adapt to life with a decreased income, as well as deteriorating health, can prevent them from cashing in life's little perks they had been putting off. The tired feet, impaired vision, and deteriorating hearing all keep them farther and farther away from the dreams they had when they were young. From when they thought they were going to have all the time and energy in the world when they retire.

WHY ON EARTH DO WE POSTPONE OUR DREAMS UNTIL RETIREMENT AGE? WHY DO WE NEED A DEFINING EVENT TO ROCK OUR LIVES IN ORDER TO KICK US INTO GEAR? WHY ARE PEOPLE AFRAID TO BET THEIR MONEY ON THE STOCK MARKET, BUT ARE WILLING TO BET THAT UPON RETIREMENT THEY WILL HAVE ENOUGH TIME, MONEY, AND GOOD HEALTH TO REALIZE EVERYTHING THEY HAVE BEEN POSTPONING?

Does this collective tendency doom us to become the heroes of *The Bucket List?* In this movie, **Morgan Freeman** and **Jack Nicholson** play two seventy-year-old cancer patients who meet in the oncology ward and decide to realize their wildest dreams before they die. They skydive, fly to Egypt, Africa, and India, participate in a road race, climb the Himalayas, laugh until they cry, get a tattoo, and live whatever time they have left completely on the edge.

Do we really have to arrive at our redemptive, life-changing epiphanies while the angel of death is already knocking on our door?

Dr. Randy Pausch, an American professor of computer science, human–computer interaction, and design at Carnegie Mellon University in Pittsburgh, Pennsylvania, died of pancreatic cancer at the age of forty-eight. When he learned that his days were numbered, he sat down to write *The Last Lecture: Really Achieving Your Childhood Dreams.*

The Last Lecture is a common practice for many professors before they retire. They give a lecture to students and colleagues where they reflect upon matters that are important to them as well as their beliefs and perceptions on life.

Pausch decided to write his last lecture and give it to his students, colleagues, and loved ones. He shared insights he had accumulated over his lifetime and left an educational legacy of his values. The lecture was recorded and is available on YouTube (with sixteen million views so far) and his book is very moving.

Don't wait for horrible news to write your "last lecture" and, more importantly, don't wait to live by it. After all, the ability to live by our principles, instead of just talking about them, is the real testament to the meaning we give our lives.

Legendary TV actor **Michael Landon**, who is well known for his role as the patriarch in the TV show *Little House on the Prairie*, also died of pancreatic cancer when he was only fifty-four years old. He said in an interview before his death:

"SOMEONE SHOULD TELL US, RIGHT AT THE START OF OUR LIVES, THAT WE ARE DYING. THEN WE MIGHT LIVE LIFE TO THE LIMIT, EVERY MINUTE OF EVERY DAY. DO IT! I SAY. WHATEVER YOU WANT TO DO, DO IT NOW! THERE ARE ONLY SO MANY TOMORROWS."

Author Robert Jackson once wrote that above every cradle hangs a tombstone, to remind us that the sand in our life's hourglass starts trickling down the second the umbilical cord is cut. People gain insights and wisdom throughout the course of their lives and when they are old enough, their vision of life can be as clear as if standing on top of a cliff, seeing it laid out before them. They are not afraid of anything, since they have nothing to lose, only gain. They live the rest of their lives, catching up on those things, big or small, that they had postponed.

A year ago I read an interview with a senior nurse in a hospice for cancer patients. In the interview she talked about her patients' last moments, her conversations with them, and the immense power they manage to muster in their last hours, in the hope of hanging on long enough to have a last farewell with their loved ones, a chance to tell them a few more loving words and to share with them a few more insights on life.

On our deathbeds, so it seems, we try to do everything that we didn't do while we could. Why does this happen? More importantly, how can we change it and do more while we still have our strength?

A few weeks ago, a good friend of mine discovered that her sixty-five-year-old mother was terminally ill and her deterioration was fast and scary. During one of their intimate conversations the daughter asked her mother, "Is there anything you regret that you didn't do in your life?"

"Not having had more flings before I married your father," her mother laughed.

Be more attentive to your heart's desires and try to realize them today instead of waiting for retirement. I do not wish to scare you, or curb your joie de vivre. I'm just encouraging you to think about your secure present as opposed to your unknown future.

LIVE YOUR LIFE RIGHT NOW!

"IT IS NOT TRUE THAT PEOPLE STOP PURSUING DREAMS BECAUSE THEY GROW OLD; THEY GROW OLD BECAUSE THEY STOP PURSUING DREAMS."

GABRIEL GARCIA MÁRQUEZ

30 | MY OWN
PERSONAL MENTOR

I've had many teachers throughout the course of my life. Some of them were my school teachers, but most are people I've met along the way. Some were authors I felt inspired by, who shared with me fascinating insights, teaching me to read between the lines. Others wrote inspirational books that had an impact on me, like **Georgene Lockwood**'s *Complete Idiot's Guide to Simple Living*. I have absorbed as much as I can from successful people I've interviewed around the world and learned by example from people who are ten or twenty years older than me, whose achievements showed me a roadmap. I have made friends with many of them despite the age difference and these friendships are really dear to my heart.

Family members are also my mentors. First of whom was and is my mother, Tamar, who (even in my trying school years) made me believe that every dream I had, I could realize. She encouraged me to follow my dreams and never give up on them.

In recent years a new teacher came into my life. You already know her. Her name is Shira and she is currently five and a half years old with a brilliant joie de vivre, a loose tooth, and a serious love of everything sweet, as well as princesses.

Shira taught me to let go of my smartphone when I'm with her. She demands that I sit and draw with her for hours on end (indirectly helping me to execute my "sign up for a drawing class" item), but most of all, she provides me with endless insights and thought-provoking moments as I watch and observe her ways.

One of these moments came when she was almost three years old. Her nursery school had organized a bonfire night on the beach.

It was a beautiful spring day, light winds were blowing, and the sun was setting on the horizon. The waves were calm and our little toddlers were very happy by the sea. They took off their clothes and ran into the water, some naked, some with their nappies on. I hadn't thought about going swimming so I didn't bring her swimsuit with me. But Shira couldn't care less. She just took off her clothes and ran along with her friends.

The kids shrieked with joy. They were jumping and running around, splashing water at each other and laughing contagiously. Suddenly I noticed some of the parents' expressions. They seemed stressed and worried. Some were yelling: "Watch out!" "Don't go any deeper!" and "I told you to stay close!"

One mother who was standing behind me even went as far as screaming to her daughter, who was playing with Shira: "Careful of the sea! You don't want to drown!"

I looked at the excited, fearless kids, and then I looked at the screaming mother again. I couldn't understand why she was introducing the horrible possibility of death and drowning to her daughter at such a tender age. True, the sea can be dangerous. Also true, kids and adults sometimes drown in rough seas. But now? The kids were wading in water not even as high as their knees and were surrounded by supervising adults. All I could think about was this horrible fear of the sea that the mother was now passing onto her daughter.

☑

Even at Shira's birth, her mother and I could already recognize some of her defining characteristics. Later on we watched her adopt the behaviors that she had observed around her: In us, in her grandparents, in her nursery school friends and teachers (both male and female).

In her first three years, Shira was a fearless child. Even today I think she is fairly brave. When she was an infant she used to pull our cat's ears and tail, stick her tiny hands into strange dogs' mouths in the park, and draw on the wall in our hallway with some talent and even more confidence.

When she was a toddler, we were always attentive to her basic needs and wants. There is something magical (though exhausting at times) about the way children so naturally expect their needs to be met right away. When Shira's friends come to play, they all, with no exception, act out of sheer emotion.

They are hyperactive and jumpy when they are pleased with something and quickly cry when something goes wrong. When I give them delicious junk food they devour it like there's no tomorrow, but when I give them healthy snacks they frown and reject them. Kids don't lie about their feelings. They are not afraid to say what is going through their minds or abide by the rules of political correctness.

They are 100 percent loyal to themselves and their feelings, they believe in magic and in fairytales and dream giant pink dreams about the future. Only recently Shira told me about her dream to one day live in a house with some of her best friends. I politely suggested she postponed her grandiose real-estate plan and we conversed about how some dreams are realistic and some are not.

Mental maturity has many advantages. The boundaries we create for ourselves as we mature are essential for retaining our values and humanity. Maturity also enables us to make a living and realize our material dreams. On the other hand, maturity also brings a bag of strict social restrictions, and rules that we apply almost always automatically center on ourselves.

☑

Being a father of two little girls, I'm very careful not to frighten them with unnecessary warnings about things they may or may not be exposed to in the future. Except for the one time Shira took a little too much interest in the wall socket.

Parenthetically I will share with you a childhood memory of my beloved grandmother, who used to mumble again and again to herself: "Life is difficult." She would say this even when returning from a designer boutique excessive shopping spree. I never found this phrase to be very inspiring and tried to correct her: "Not hard, interesting!" She passed away a year ago at the age of eighty-five, after having lived with Alzheimer's disease for almost ten years.

So with this in the back of my mind, I try to raise Shira and Noga in relative serenity. I enjoy talking to Shira about Planet Earth, nature, and art, and avoid exposing her to life's less photogenic sides. She will have enough time to face life's difficulties.

Babies first come into this world as a clean slate, with no sense of shame or fear, and are mainly affected by the behavior of the adults around them. They imitate and assimilate it until it becomes second nature. Do children with cowardly parents become cowardly adults? Unfortunately, in most cases, the answer is yes. We pass on our fears and our childhood traumas to our children. If we were yelled at for cutting up a curtain in the living room or for drawing on the bedroom wall, they will sense our responses and learn to restrain themselves accordingly. We convey, without realizing it, the anger and disappointment our parents passed on to us, to the point of suppressing our children's life energy.

31 | WHAT DO WE LOSE ON THE WAY FROM CHILDHOOD TO MATURITY?

Why is it that the older we become, the more we let people around us project their fears on us and stifle our dreams?

Why do we believe the pessimists telling us that it's not possible? That you can't make a living out of art—though I know quite a few who have earned millions from their art. Or even those who say it's too dangerous. True, some have died on their way to the top of Everest, but for the most part people make it back safely to share their experience. They may even tell you that you're going to regret it later. Trust me when I tell you that you'll always regret not having done it even more.

Why is it that over the years, most of us turn from brave, fearless children into overly calculating and hesitant creatures, humbly carrying the fear we inherited from our parents, grandparents, or peers, or even ourselves? Why is it that as we grow older, we smother our creativity and courage and come up with all sorts of excuses instead?

"I have a family now, I don't have time to dream."

"I'm too old for this childish behavior."

"I'm a senior manager, it's not appropriate for a man my age to behave like that."

"I have a mortgage. I can't quit my job and lose a steady salary just to open the business I've been dreaming about my whole life."

"I'm past the age when I can make a fool out of myself."

These are just some of the thoughts that go through our heads when we ponder our hidden dreams. People get addicted to their excuses and prefer to chain themselves to what exists rather than to what could be.

More than once I have heard from agents and managers, who were responsible for my career either as an actor, a journalist, or an author, that I should be very careful in choosing my next step. More than once I found myself arguing with them as they tried to prevent me from accepting a job, or tried to convince me to turn down an offer claiming that it was wrong for my brand.

I kept asking: "What about the path that I need to walk? What about having new experiences? What about making mistakes so that I can learn?"

One of my former agents once explained to me that I needed to think as a brand and not to give in to my emotional whims. I explained that my name was Yuval Abramovitz, not Coca-Cola, and we parted on friendly terms.

As an artist who has entrusted his career to the hands of many professional managers along the way, I can say with certainty that no one can represent me as well as I can represent myself.

Over the years, I found many people who believed in me and in my ideas, but never as much as I believed in myself.

DON'T PLACE THE OUTCOMES OF DREAMS IN THE HANDS OF OTHERS.

DO YOU HAVE A DREAM? ONLY YOU CAN DRIVE IT FORWARD IF YOU TRULY WANT IT. WHY DO WE ASK CHILDREN WHAT THEY WANT TO BE WHEN THEY GROW UP, BUT STOP ASKING THEM WHEN THEY REACH OLDER AGE? DO WE HAVE NOTHING TO ASPIRE TO ONCE WE GROW UP?

Some of my friends think I'm a brave man. Well, I'm not as brave as rock climbers, skydivers, or people who swim with sharks (I'm no fan of any activity that doesn't take place on solid ground), but I am brave enough to follow my heart's desires.

That last bit is only partly true.

I do not encourage the hasty behavior that comes from not adequately thinking things through. At the same time, I don't support people being passive to the point where their lives are ruled by extreme caution. I learned from experience that risk-taking and courage are muscles that you can train.

I have done a lot of things in my life that required a certain amount of courage. When I started acting in theatre and television, I performed in front of hundreds of thousands of viewers. I wrote books and dared to tell the world: "Here is something worth reading, paying for, and spending precious time on." I established businesses, some more successful than others. And here I am now, Yuval, born into a normal middle-class family, writing a book in the hope that it will inspire readers around the world, even though many self-help books are written by tycoons, publicity experts, economists, and experts in their own fields.

Where do I get the courage to do it all? What helps me silence the negative voices in my head and threaten to weaken my willpower? Do I think I'm a little insolent?

Truth is I'm rattling with fear and I think I'm probably pretty insolent. But then I do have fears of failure and humiliation. Fears of aiming too high, of over-shooting the mark. Over the years I have lost some of my audacity and become a more careful and calculated man.

"A careful man is the coward's cousin" is a taunt that reminds me of the brash impulsiveness of my teenage years. It reminds me of the careful consideration I take when assessing every professional or personal step. "I have two daughters to take care of." "I already have an audience which expects my usual familiar shtick." "It's not appropriate at my age." "It may lead to some doors shutting in my face." I admit that in my younger years I was less careful and much more attentive to the whims of my heart. In moments when fear takes over, I remind myself of the brave boy I used to be.

When starting out as a writer, I wrote for a website where the owner consistently wouldn't pay me on time. At the time I was trying to establish my career as a journalist, writing for nine different newspapers, and drafting copy for competing websites, all under different pseudonyms. So I didn't pay too much attention to it. One day, I noticed that I had received my last paycheck from the website nine months earlier. I called the owner's office and his secretary explained that he was sick, abroad, or else too busy to sign my paycheck. I went on to speak to his accountant who came up with a few more excuses to explain why I had not been paid. Eventually, I managed to get the owner's email address and sent him a request to pay me. His answer was very generic, that my appeals had gone to his spam folder. He promised to send my check along with interest and compensation.

The promised check arrived two months and three reminders later. The check was postdated for two months later. In other words, I was paid for my work after more than a year! I was furious and decided to take a little revenge.

The day I deposited the check into my account, I wrote a harsh letter explaining that this was no way to treat an employee, especially a young journalist who was trying to set his life on track. I signed it with a little note at the bottom: "PS, to make sure you get my email, I am sending a copy of this letter to every one of your employees." That was, without a doubt, hasty, bold, and very stupid.

Over the years, that website owner has become a senior and very influential media figure. It was clear to me, as I assumed that it was to him, that we were never going to work together again. Life, however, sometimes has its own plans.

One day I got a call from an editor I used to work with. She informed me that this media figure I had once publicly shamed had a new media project and that I was wanted for his team.

"I assume you don't know about our history." I laughed awkwardly. I told her the story and she agreed that there was a problem, and that she might not be able to hire me for the job. Two days later, she called saying there was no problem. "We didn't talk about your past and he thinks you are the right person for the job."

I met him face to face when I arrived to discuss my employment contract. He shook my hand, wished me luck and said, "I like people who stand their ground." We both knew what he was talking about and I immediately took the opportunity to apologize for my indignant letter. But this proved my theory that being true to yourself, in spite of the possible consequences, is perceived as a positive trait.

I probably wouldn't do the same thing again today; I'm much more cautious and calculating. I have matured and maturity, as I've said before, has its faults, especially when paralyzes and stifles our will.

32 | MEETING THE CHILDREN WE WERE

In some of my first lectures I asked the audience to blow up balloons that I had placed under their chairs with their eyes covered, then to blow soap bubbles, dance the chicken dance, play hopscotch, and jump rope with one of their hands or legs tied. Then I asked if they knew why I wanted them to do those things. Here are some of the great answers I received:

✔ To prove to us that we can do things under restraints and limitations.

✔ To train our brain.

✔ To get us out of our comfort zone.

✔ To challenge us.

✔ To activate different areas in the brain (like when writing with your non dominant-hand).

✔ To prove to us that exercise enables us to do things we didn't know how to do.

I heard many excellent and wise answers, though only a few people got my real, yet simple, reason.

The truth was that I just wanted to make them feel like children again, if only for a few moments. I wanted to encourage them to do something without a purpose or a goal. Just for the sake of having fun. I wanted to remind them that sometimes you can do things without thinking about the consequences and without knowing what the results are going to be. I wanted them to giggle, fall, even get hurt a bit, and those experiences were exactly what happened after we played those silly games.

I love meeting people who have kept their inner child.

One of my recent young acquaintances who unbeknownst to him inspired me is Omri Hayun.

Hayun is a twenty-three-year-old gossip blogger. He started out at the age of seventeen and the first scoop he had back in 2009 exposed the problems in the filtering process for Israel's major TV singing competition reality show *A Star Is Born*. That was the scoop that brought him notoriety. He exposed the fact that one of the contestants was still a minor and below the competing age. Hayun's scoop led the contestant to leave the show the following day. He became Israeli media's "it man" overnight. His new status resulted in "hot" information traveling his way and he began revealing behind-the-scenes secrets of numerous TV series and reality shows.

When he prematurely exposed the five final contestants of an extremely popular reality TV show, the executives of the Channel 2 Network threatened him with a lawsuit. I interviewed him back then and asked if he was afraid to be dragged into a courtroom for this little trick. Hayun looked at me and grinned. "For what offense, exactly? For having published a spoiler? For revealing secrets from a reality show?"

I don't always agree with the items that Hayun chooses to publish in his blog, but it continues to operate and even to make some profit when he exposes big stories.

When I interviewed him I felt as if I had already heard his words before from someone else. I had a feeling I knew that person well. That night, at home, I realized who he reminded me of: Hayun's courage reminded me of the courage I once had, before I became more "premeditated," "dignified," and "esteemed" and before I started to care what people said about me.

A few weeks after interviewing Hayun and spending some time looking for a topic for a blog, *The List* concept came to mind and I set out on my journey.

I published my list of dreams without thinking about what people might think about my aspirations for a slim body or meeting Oprah. My list and nothing but my list was in front of my eyes, or more accurately, mine and the thousand other eyes that could help me realize my aspirations. At the same time, I promised myself that I was going to let my inner child continue doing what his heart desires.

DARE!

GO WILD, SUPRISE YOURSELF
AND THE PEOPLE AROUND YOU,

AND DON'T HESITATE TO ASK FOR HELP!

THINK BIG,

THINK
HUGE!

IF YOU OCCUPY YOUR MIND WITH PETTY THOUGHTS, YOU MAY LOSE THE BIGGER PICTURE.

33 | WHEN DARING
MEETS AN ACCURATE MESSAGE

During the process of writing this book, I visited Berlin for the annual film festival and had coffee with a young Canadian movie producer. He excitedly and proudly told me how he managed to sign the Oscar-winning actress, Emma Thompson, for a small independent movie he was about to produce.

"It must have been hard to get her," I said.

"Much easier than you would expect," he answered. "I sent the script to her agent. He answered that it would take her about six weeks to answer, but within three days she got back in touch saying she would do the film. Apparently, although she was swamped with scripts, she was eager for a different and challenging part. I've also managed to snare some of Britain's most established actors."

"Do you know what I have learned from your case?" I asked him. "That even the busiest, most successful people seek out challenges and excitement, and a lot of times we wrong them and ourselves by presuming they are too busy.

"In the end, everyone has interests," he answered, smiling. "Mine is to find the best actors and enable them to experience a new professional challenge."

☑

Another story of courage and audacity came to me from a well-known businessman, and it took place in a burger bar.

"One day," he told me, "as I was sitting with my family over lunch in a restaurant, a young woman approached the table and asked for my permission to interrupt my lunch. I was sitting there with my family— all of us were chewing our hamburgers. She introduced herself as a beginner in PR and told me that she had been following my work and said how much she was impressed by my work. She then put herself forward as the best candidate for a PR position on one of my projects.

"Her audacity in interrupting my lunch with the wife and kids to promote herself for the job, in spite of her lack of experience, impressed me very much but at the time, I was working with a very well-known and expensive PR person. I told that young woman that at the moment I didn't need any additional staff, but I would gladly consider hiring her in the future."

"And did you ever hire her?" I asked.

"Absolutely! A few months later when I was considering refreshing my staff, my already-expensive PR person demanded a substantial raise. I remembered that young woman who 'bothered' me in the restaurant, and thought that with her boldness and drive, she would probably not hesitate to 'bother' senior editors in the media on my behalf. I called her, and I wasn't wrong. She's now giving her heart and soul to this job. Her work is impressive and my businesses get twice the exposure they used to get."

☑

Stories like this teach us that boldness, which is perceived by many as impudence, is a rare and desired trait in both dreamers and realizers.

During many advisory meetings with senior managers, I learned about the considerations they take into account when they hire a new employee. They favor prowess, enthusiasm, and creativity over experience and recommendations. "Many have experience; only a few have prowess," the owner of one of the biggest real estate companies in Israel told me.

YES, PROWESS AND COURAGE CONNECT DREAMERS TO ONE ANOTHER. THEY REMIND EACH OTHER OF THE BOLD CHILDREN THAT THEY ONCE WERE, AND THAT THEY MAY HAVE LOST DURING LIFE'S JOURNEY.

Just recently, my good friend Michal Shreiber, owner of a successful Internet marketing firm, told me about an old dream she had—to work with the successful American author Richard Bach, who wrote the best-seller *Jonathan Livingston Seagull*. For years she had been dreaming about meeting him. A quick Google search revealed the email address of his editor. Michal wrote to the editor and concisely told her about herself and her dream to meet and work with Bach. A day later, she received a response, and two weeks later, Michal found herself boarding a plane to Las Vegas to meet her revered writer. They are now exploring an option of working on a mutual project on the Internet, although she will be working from Israel while he is in the USA.

Another such powerful story found its way into *The List* mailbox. A woman told me about a dream she had realized long before the Internet era. Here is **Tzipi Nave**'s story, as she wrote it to the blog:

When I was twenty years old, I admired Woody Allen. It was way back in the eighties, when he was at the peak of his cinematic fame. I decided that I wanted to meet him and it was clear to me that I couldn't do it as a groupie. I knew I needed to raise an interest in him to meet me. I had to offer him a significant conversation that would be interesting for him just as much as it would be for me. I was then finishing my Bachelor of Arts in Psychology and Communication at the Hebrew University in Jerusalem.

I had a cinema professor who split his time working in Jerusalem half of the year and in New York the other half as a director of documentaries. He suggested that I work with him. I finished my degree, submitting a thesis titled: "Dealing With Fear of Death as Reflected in The Films of Woody Allen." I went with my professor to New York and decided to send my research to Allen's agent, along with a letter telling him I was from Israel and would really like to talk to the director. I told him about my research, wrote that I thought it would interest Allen, and would he be happy to meet me to discuss it.

A week and a half after I sent my research to Allen's agent, I received a letter from Mr. Allen himself, suggesting that I come to Michael's Pub, where he used to play his clarinet every Monday. He invited me to join him for dinner after the show. And so I did. We came to the pub, listened to Allen play, joined him for dinner, and had a long conversation. That was twenty-five years ago, long before the Internet, and already I understood a few things about realizing dreams.

That story made me smile, partly because I also like Woody Allen's films very much and would later meet him twice at the Cannes Film Festival. I got to ask him about the motivation behind his creations and dreams with his answer being that if he didn't have another movie to make, he'd start thinking about his age and about death. But mostly it made me smile because I suddenly realized that some of my personal appeals, such as the ones to Oprah and to the Australian authorities, were not reasoned, focused, challenging, or interesting enough for the other side. They were missing the element of counter value that the helping party should be getting out of the transaction. The value of satisfaction, the benefit of advertisement, or some information that I could deliver. Not everybody dreams of meeting movie stars or successful singers. Some have more practical dreams like a promotion at work, starting a relationship, or improving their health.

Have you ever spoken about those dreams to your boss? Does he know anything about your great, secret aspirations regarding your workplace? Did you share your suggestions for improving efficiency? Did you express your future goals to him? Did you talk to him about that two-month vacation that you're fantasizing about taking in the middle of your life? Or maybe you are one of those silent people who are afraid to talk to your boss because he might think that you're undermining him? What is actually stopping you from expressing your professional dreams to your boss? One day he will need to fill an important position. Why would he think of you if you have never shared your professional dreams?

Imagine that you're working in a huge conglomerate with thousands of employees, and the CEO is some kind of a legendary figure, sitting in the ivory tower of management—a distant CEO, whose name frequently appears in the gossip pages of the financial newspapers. Now imagine that you are in the elevator in the building where you work, and they walk in. You have twenty floors and thirty seconds to spend together in the elevator. What would you do? What would you say to them other than "Hello"? Could you tell them your dream accurately and succinctly?

WHAT IF YOU MET BILL GATES, ONE OF THE RICHEST, MOST POWERFUL PEOPLE IN THE WORLD IN AN ELEVATOR? WOULD YOU BE ABLE TO QUICKLY EXPRESS YOURSELF AND TELL HIM ABOUT YOUR DREAM SO THAT MAYBE HE WOULD HELP YOU REALIZE IT?

34 | BRUCE WILLIS
AND I

In the last few years I have been exposed to hundreds of people's "bravery" stories, while my own career has also been dotted with special and exciting moments that came about thanks to a bold, whimsical spirit, playing the odds and taking risks.

This is how I found myself sitting down to dinner with Mr. Bruce Willis in Paris, in a restaurant on the Champs-Élysées. In 2010, I arrived in Paris as a reporter for *Israel Today* for a press conference with Mr. Willis, who was promoting a Polish Vodka brand he had shares in. Early in the afternoon, I bustled into position, with twenty other French reporters and waited for "Mr. Die Hard" to speak. Only Mr. Willis, who had arrived at the event straight from another press conference somewhere in Europe, was too exhausted to talk all that much. After twenty minutes of mundane questions asked by reporters who were too polite for their own good, I found I had too little for a real article. Four empty pages and a front cover photo slot were waiting for me back at *Israel Today*, and my story was doomed.

I found out the PR person for the vodka brand's Israeli importer had received invitations for a dinner party with Mr. Willis that night. So I pulled her aside and strongly suggested that I should join her at the event. I needed an article and she needed publicity.

That evening, we arrived at a fancy restaurant in the Champs-Élysées where the event took place. It was full of business people and Parisian celebrities. Mr. Willis sat with his entourage in a remote corner and was surrounded by bodyguards.

"If he gets up, I'm getting an interview," I told the PR person who was sitting with me at the table.

"How are you going to do that?" she asked.

"I don't know yet." I grinned. "I'm just going to ask him."

I waited for an opportunity and when I saw him get up and walk toward a group of business people, I approached him and said: "Hello Bruce, my name is Yuval and I'm a reporter from Israel, and I really need your help."

He looked at me and smiled. "How can I help you?"

"I write for the most popular newspaper in Israel and I'm supposed to return home with a cover story about you. The problem is that I don't have enough material from the press conference, so I thought maybe I could sit next to you at dinner and casually interview you."

He gave me a long look and winked. "I'll try to help you, but first I'd be happy if you helped me by taking care of lowering the volume of the music in here."

I immediately located the owner and asked him to turn the music down. I went back to my table and sat biting my nails while looking at Bruce's table.

After fifteen minutes, his personal manager approached us and said, "Mr. Willis wants to invite you to join him at his table." We sat in front of him, extremely excited, and discovered a kind, warm, and open man who told me about his second marriage, his daughter who was studying archeology and who would soon be traveling to Israel for a dig. He even revealed some insights from his years as an actor in Hollywood.

Meeting Mr. Willis has taught me one of the most important lessons of my life about courage and the power of the word "help" in opening hearts and iron gates.

WHEN WE SAY TO SOMEONE THE WORDS "I NEED HELP," WE ARE BASICALLY GIVING SOMEONE A CHANCE TO PROVE THEIR POWER TO US AND TO THEMSELVES.

Who doesn't like to show that they can be strong and capable? You don't need to be John McClane to help people. You can help people by offering a tip, some of your time, or a quick and easy click on the "share" button on a social network. So write down your dreams and ask for help, but make sure you also respond with as much proactive kindness as you can when other request help from you.

35 | HELPING IS FUN

A lot of the education we receive encourages us to fend for ourselves and to not to ask for help or burden those around us. As good students of our parents, family, and teachers, we enthusiastically adopt messages we are taught. Don't ask for help, don't bother others, and do our best to manage on our own.

I know quite a few people who have suffered with big problems over many years and still haven't asked for help. Someone I worked with several years ago got into heavy financial debt. I repeatedly suggested he talk about it with people, ask for their help, and share his delicate situation with his suppliers and employees. But his ego wouldn't allow him. Within two years, he was so deep in debt that he lost both his business and his home.

Why shouldn't we ask others for help? What do we have to lose? What are we so afraid of, a momentary humiliation? Or that someone will think our dreams are stupid? When I am asked why the world has responded to my list, my answer is clear: I simply asked. I insisted on shouting my dreams instead of letting them remain silent. I overcame the classical conditioning that encourages us to fend for ourselves and not to burden others, in case they are burdened with their own troubles. I dared to stand up and say, "Dear world, I will not be able to get where I want to by myself. I need you to help me up the mountain of my dreams."

LIFE OFFERS US MANY DIFFERENT PATHS. WE CAN CHOOSE THE MAIN ONE—THE ONE MOST PEOPLE WALK. IT'S WELL-LIT, MODERN, SAFE, AND MAY LEAD US TO OUR DESIRED GOAL—BUT IT IS VERY CROWDED AND JAMMED.

AT THE SAME TIME, THERE ARE OTHER PATHS. SOME ARE NARROW, DARK, AND FULL OF POTHOLES. DANGERS MAY LURK ON THESE BACK ROADS, BUT IF YOU OVERCOME THE FEAR OF THESE OBSTACLES AND THE FEAR OF THE DARKNESS, YOU MAY REACH YOUR GOAL FASTER BECAUSE THERE ARE NOT MANY PEOPLE ON THESE ROADS.

I like to take the side roads and think outside the box. I prefer a direct approach to the director, the casting director, the CEO, the publisher, the businessman, or any other significant person. I tend to avoid the middleman who will never convey my message with the same accuracy, passion, and enthusiasm as I can.

Much to my surprise, I discovered that no matter your rank or seniority, people like to be addressed naturally and appreciate the fact that you see them as a person and not as an icon.

In one of my lectures, a thirty-year-old woman talked about her dream to write a political television series. She had invested a lot of energy into it, taking screenwriting courses and private lessons with political speechwriters and reading dozens of political biographies as part of her research. She had written two episodes, the synopses for a several more, and a logline. The only thing left to do was send her script off to some senior figures in the TV industry.

I offered her my email address and told her I would send her some of my contacts in the entertainment industry.

"Really?" She couldn't believe it. "Do you really mean it?"

"Yes, why are you so surprised?"

"Because it's an enormous help," she said, hugging me.

That night she emailed me thanking me for my generosity. She received an invitation to pitch her idea at one of the television channels in Israel and once again thanked me. Gratitude is wonderful but a willingness to ask for help is a blessing as well. Teach yourself to ask for help and be willing to accept help from total strangers. Most people are happy to help, even when there's no direct benefit for them.

☑

The manager of one of my businesses has writer's block and dreams about writing her second play. Her first play was performed in a festival for short plays, winning several prizes and receiving warm reviews.

One day I introduced her to a close friend who happens to be a creative writing teacher. He heard her problem and offered to meet her in a café and try to help her break through her writer's block.

"You told him to help me, right?" she asked.

"I had no idea he was meeting you," I replied. "It's great that he is volunteering his time and sharing his expertise with you."

"Have you paid him? Will he expect money for helping me out?"

She couldn't believe that a professional would be willing to spend an hour of their time to help others. She kept looking for the catch.

Our difficulty in asking for help, as well as the difficulty in receiving it, sometimes overpowers our logic. Irrational fear takes over and paralyzes us. We also fear straying from the secure and familiar road.

A few years ago I shot a pilot for a talk show—"host a talk show"—is an item on my new list, which you can find at the end of this book. My agent connected me with a senior producer who loved the idea and was willing to risk the financial expense to shoot the pilot. We found a channel that was interested in purchasing the pilot and after a few months we were given a time slot in the channel's programming schedule. We were then informed that the airing of the show would have to be postponed for a few months due to budget constraints.

After a year, I asked my agent to send the pilot to a few more channels before it became too old.

"It's not a good time," she answered. "Everybody's having financial problems and there's no demand for talk shows at the moment. We should wait for the right moment."

I know she only wanted what was best for me, but she was acting in conventional ways—remember, the older we get and the more "experience" we gain, the more we tend to act in predictable ways.

I tried to remind her that a little audacity and thinking outside the box never hurt anybody. I wanted to send the pilot to all the channels at the same time. The worst-case scenario would be a blanket rejection, and if that was the case I would understand that it was time to shelve the project and start developing a new one.

Eventually I sent the pilot to a few media channels, including several Internet sites (even back then the Internet was challenging traditional television networks) and within a month, I received two positive responses to start discussions. My idea is slowly taking shape and will become a reality.

FORGET YOUR FEARS.
IT'S BETTER TO DARE, TO BE UNIQUE, TO SHARE, AND TO DREAM. YOU HAVE ALMOST
NOTHING TO LOSE, AND EVERYTHING TO GAIN.

? | EXERCISE

? Talk to people whose work you admire, find out how they have reached their goals. What original steps did they take along the way? When did they have to use some "chutzpah" in order to get ahead?

? Write five things that you have achieved in your life by thinking out of the box. I'm sure you will find out you are much braver than you thought.

36 ARE YOU READY TO WRITE?
LET'S GO!

The first half of this book as been a warm-up for your brain and a chance for you to arrive at the same conclusions I have regarding an effective writing. Now, let me lead you down the road to make your own lists.

A LIST IS NOT A RANDOM SCRIBBLE ON A PIECE OF PAPER. IT REQUIRES THOROUGH THINKING, SORTING, AND ESPECIALLY PRECISION.

This is my time to stop talking and invite you to write your own list of dreams. Grab some paper and write your lists over and over again until you reach a final, refined list that will guide you in the coming months.

Take a pencil, an eraser, and a glass of wine (or any other favorite beverage) and set up a relaxing environment. Sit down in your yard, on your roof, your balcony, the beach, or under a warm cover. Turn off the phone, the computer, or any other beeping distraction. Concentrate. Most importantly remove all boundaries, inhibitions, and barriers and let yourself dream.

A LIST IS A CONTRACT WITH YOURSELF, REMEMBER?

In order to accurately write your list, dedicate an appropriate amount of time, just as you would if you went to consult with a lawyer who was charging you a fortune for every minute of his time.

37 | STARTING THE JOURNEY

First, pour out every dream you have onto the paper.

Try to reach a list of 100 dreams, including tasks, desires, and goals.

Those can be small and insignificant, like fixing the hole in the kitchen wall, or using that gift card that has been lying in your purse for six months, or getting a new haircut.

Look for dreams and goals of all kinds. The small and the personal, the big and the universal, business goals and social goals.

Don't continue reading this book until you complete your list of 100 goals, even if it takes you more than an hour. Even if you have to set the book aside in order to think, you can return to reading it in a few days. This is not an easy task.

DO NOT SKIP THIS STAGE AND DO NOT CUT THE PROCESS SHORT.

As *The List* spread to new audiences, I received more and more enthusiastic responses. There were however, people who expressed reservations about the idea. More than once I found myself having a semantic argument about the definition of "dream."

"The idea of managing a list is great, and guiding people to break it down into little steps is really positive," said a psychologist who attended one of my lectures. "But you are misleading people when you ask them to shout out their dreams. A dream is something that by its very nature is unattainable."

"But in the twenty-first century, in the era of social networking, you can achieve almost anything. People are already talking about booking round trips to space," I answered.

"A dream is a fantasy," explained a different psychologist.

"I still think fantasies are attainable, as long as they are realistic in relation to our specific circumstances. Other than a force majeure causing us to stop or a lack of talent, I truly believe that it's all in our hands," I insisted. "It was Simone de Beauvoir who said that the fastest way of getting rid of a fantasy is to make it come true."

After another psychologist noted "a dream is not attainable," I went to my bookshelf and pulled out a dictionary and looked for the definition of the word "dream."

Hope. Yearning. The words jumped out of the book. I looked in more dictionaries and found some more definitions. A night vision. An imaginary sight that a person sees in their sleep. Imagination. Illusion. I didn't find anywhere that a dream is unattainable and of course I didn't find any reference to the claim that someone who dares to dream and speak about their dreams is unrealistic. Throughout human history there have been thousands who dared to dream and sell their dream to see it come true.

I suppose that as *The List* gains popularity, so too will the opposition to it, exactly because it is so simple. People often think that they need complex solutions or hang on to the excuse that they don't have the means or resources to untangle their own situations. I suggest that they just take a pen and paper and write, and then shout, and shout, and shout.

We are the world champions at finding excuses for why our dreams are unattainable. Instead, it would be much better if we explored ways to reach our goals. We would have crossed so many items off our lists.

If you do not identify with the word "dream," here are some different words for you: "Shout your desires/goals/aspirations/thoughts!" Someone is bound to hear you eventually.

I don't care what you want to call it, as long as you achieve it.

THIS IS A PRACTICAL EXERCISE. USE IT AND BENEFIT FROM IT.

Having a free and open mind when writing lists helps us find dreams we weren't aware we even had.

"How weird! I wrote on my list that I wanted to learn Thai boxing," said a slender woman. "I don't even know why I wrote it!"

A short conversation about her dreams revealed that she was developing a workshop on female empowerment when suddenly she had an epiphany—physical activity is a wonderful way to demonstrate just how much our sense of strength depends on the strength of our body. Twenty-four hours after writing her list, she was sweating it out at boxing practice.

A young actor wrote of an aspiration to throw out all of the clothes in his wardrobe and start to dress properly. He had the idea of offering his services as a presenter for fashion blogs, in return for clothes and styling services from them.

When I complimented him on his great idea, he answered, "I had never thought of such a thing until you encouraged me to remove all the blocks and barriers and write down all of my dreams. After I did, it just started to pour out of me."

So there you have it! There is no trick or magic—just dedicate the time to yourself. Remove all the barriers you have put up over all those years and set your list free.

Don't use excuses like it is impossible, I don't have time, or I don't have money. No more explanations like my husband won't let me, or my wife needs money for the house. Just let your heart and mind feel the pages.

HAVE A SUCCESSFUL WRITING EXPERIENCE!

"A JOURNEY OF A THOUSAND MILES BEGINS WITH A SINGLE STEP."

LAO TZU

1.

2.

3.

4.

5.

6.

7.

8.

9.

10.

"VISION WITHOUT ACTION IS DAY DREAMING. ACTION WITHOUT A VISION IS A NIGHTMARE."

CHINESE PROVERB

11.

12.

13.

14.

15.

16.

17.

18.

19.

20.

"PEOPLE WITHOUT FANTASIES DON'T DO FANTASTIC THINGS."

SHIMON PERES

21.

22.

23.

24.

25.

26.

27.

28.

29.

30.

"EACH MAN'S LIFE REPRESENTS THE ROAD TOWARD HIMSELF, AND ATTEMPT AT SUCH A ROAD, THE INTIMATION OF A PATH."

HERMANN HESSE

31.

32.

33.

34.

35.

36.

37.

38.

39.

40.

"SOME PEOPLE WANT IT TO HAPPEN, SOME WISH IT WOULD HAPPEN, AND OTHERS MAKE IT HAPPEN."

MICHAEL JORDAN

41.

42.

43.

44.

45.

46.

47.

48.

49.

50.

"DOUBT KILLS MORE DREAMS THAN FAILURE EVER WILL."

UNKNOWN

51.

52.

53.

54.

55.

56.

57.

58.

59.

60.

"REMEMBERING THAT YOU ARE GOING TO DIE ONE DAY IS THE BEST WAY TO AVOID THE TRAP OF THINKING YOU HAVE SOMETHING TO LOSE."

STEVE JOBS

61.

62.

63.

64.

65.

66.

67.

68.

69.

70.

"THERE ARE NO SECRETS TO SUCCESS. IT IS THE RESULT OF PREPARATION, HARD WORK, AND LEARNING FROM FAILURE."

COLIN POWELL

71.

72.

73.

74.

75.

76.

77.

78.

79.

80.

"FOR ME, LIFE IS CONTINUOUSLY BEING HUNGRY. THE MEANING OF LIFE IS NOT SIMPLY TO EXIST, TO SURVIVE, BUT TO MOVE AHEAD, TO GO UP, TO ACHIEVE, TO CONQUER."

ARNOLD SCHWARZENEGGER

81.

82.

83.

84.

85.

86.

87.

88.

89.

90.

"IF YOU DON'T BUILD YOUR DREAM, SOMEONE WILL HIRE YOU TO HELP BUILD THEIRS."

TONY GASKINS

91.

92.

93.

94.

95.

96.

97.

98.

99.

100.

GOOD JOB!

YOU ARE NOW HOLDING A FULL AND DIVERSE LIST OF DREAMS.

Go over it, read it carefully, and try to answer with utmost honesty:

✔ **Do you clearly understand why you wrote each and every item in the list?**

✔ **Are there items in it that in retrospect surprise you?**

✔ **Can you find a common denominator running through your dreams?**

✔ **Are there any items that make you want to start promoting them right now?**

✔ **Which items in your list do you want to achieve the most (in the long run, too) and can begin promoting right now?**

IF YOU HAVE ANSWERS FOR THE LAST TWO QUESTIONS, START TO WORK TO PROMOTE THESE GOALS—RIGHT NOW! IF YOU DON'T HAVE SATISFACTORY ANSWERS, LET'S FIND WAYS TO ACHIEVE AT LEAST A PART OF YOUR LIST.

---

38 | WHAT I HAVE LEARNED ABOUT ACHIEVING DREAMS

You are now but a few steps away from your final draft of your refined list.

Along my *The List* journey I have learned many things, but especially this: In order to realize a list of dreams, we have to be full of positive energy and power. We must believe, even in the face of the hardships and obstacles that we will encounter along the way, that we are able to achieve our dreams.

In the next part of the book, I will share with you all of the knowledge that I have accumulated to help you keep refining your lists, but mostly to help you stay in high gear while moving forward.

One of the problems with inspirational books (I have read many) and empowerment workshops (I have participated in a few of these too) is that the readers or listeners finish them enthusiastic and motivated to make some kind of a change in their lives, but after a week or so the enthusiasm fades away and they are stuck in the same old routines.

DO NOT GIVE UP ON YOURSELF THIS TIME.

? | EXERCISE

Pick one item from your list of 100 dreams. Go to your computer right now and start Googling ways to realize your dream. Take your smartphone and text ten of your friends asking for help to realize your dream. Committing, in front of others, helps dreams come true. Don't let your enthusiasm fade away. Take the first step of your journey right now! Don't put it off for later. Do not let negative thoughts such as "this will never happen for me" or "I don't like bothering others" take over.

IN ORDER TO KEEP HIGH LEVELS OF ENERGY, CHARGE YOURSELF WITH AS MANY INSPIRATIONAL STORIES AS POSSIBLE. I READ DOZENS OF INSPIRATIONAL BOOKS EVERY YEAR FROM AROUND THE WORLD: BOOKS WRITTEN BY POLITICIANS, BUSINESSMEN, PHILOSOPHERS, RESEARCHERS, AND PSYCHOLOGISTS.

ADOPT THIS HABIT EVEN IF YOU SOMETIMES FEEL LIKE THEY ALL REPEAT THE SAME MESSAGE BUT IN DIFFERENT GUISES. IT'S ENOUGH TO FIND ONE STRONG SENTENCE WITHIN EACH ONE OF THEM THAT WILL MOTIVATE YOU TO ACT, OR A REMINDER OF SOMETHING THAT YOU HAVE READ BEFORE AND WILL STRENGTHEN YOU, TO MAKE READING WORTH IT.

39 | FORGET ABOUT IT.
IT'S BEEN DONE BEFORE
(THAT'S JUST IT—IT HASN'T BEEN DONE BEFORE!)

In my creative writing lectures I talk about how a script that I wrote based on my first novel found its way to an Israeli director who participated in productions for HBO (which is responsible for shows like *The Sopranos* and *Sex and the City*) and she invited me to turn it into a series for the network.

One of the reasons it didn't eventuate into a series was that my eldest daughter was born and I wasn't emotionally or physically ready to enter into a new and consuming adventure, which demanded my complete devotion to the process of adapting the script for an American audience. I nipped my internal negative dialogue in the bud, knowing that another opportunity would show up when I truly wanted it, but mostly when I was mentally and professionally ready for it.

After one of my lectures, in which I had told this story to an audience of teenagers, I found an email waiting for me in my inbox. "I have also written series in English," said one of the girls who attended the lecture, "and my dream is for my series to be purchased by HBO. What do you suggest that I do?"

"Google their website," I suggested, "and send the script to as many executive producers in the company as you find. Try to contact them through their personal Facebook page as well."

"But what are the chances they will even pay attention to me?" she wondered. "Millions of people must send in scripts."

"This is where you're wrong. Millions of people are certain that millions of people send them scripts and therefore don't even try. In reality, only thousands, if not hundreds, actually do it. You have nothing to lose."

PEOPLE ARE SURE THAT OTHERS HAVE BEATEN THEM TO THE PUNCH WITH A BOLD MOVE, ALTHOUGH IN REALITY ONLY A FEW TAKE THAT STEP AND GET WHAT THEY WANT.

Hundreds of the emails, sent to my blog by strangers, expressed concern about the bold step they were supposed to take and, more specifically, the fears and barriers that prevent them from taking that step.

A young singer wrote about his performances in front of audiences, the good responses and praise he had attracted, his thousands of Facebook followers—and that he had been dreaming of being signed by a major record label.

"Go and film your concert. Send a copy of the DVD or a link of the film to all the key people at the record labels. Send it to music producers who are connected to those labels. If you send your concert to 100 people, I believe that at least one of them will take a few minutes to listen to it, even if they are swamped with material that's sent to them every week. It's their job after all, among other things, to discover new talent. However, don't forget that today, artists can raise the money to produce an album directly from their audience without a need for any mediators."

As I was writing that response to him, I couldn't help remembering Mariah Carey's story of how she ran into Tommy Mottola, president of Columbia Records, at a social event and gave him one of her demo tapes. Mottola listened to it later that night on his way home and was amazed by her vocal abilities. He tracked her down and signed her up for an unprecedented contract of seven albums, changing her life forever.

I can elaborate on dozens of incidents when I was bold and it paid off, like that time I sent a personal letter to the editor of a new newspaper at his home address and was hired the next day. About how I dared to ask a theatre producer to audition for an entire new role.

One day I read in the paper about a production of a new *Fame*-inspired television series starring the first winner of *Israeli Idol*. I somehow found the director's private email (it was before Facebook), told him who I was (at the time—a relatively unknown actor with a few years' experience), and asked for an audition. He replied within an hour. Yes, one of the busiest TV producers in Israel found the time to reply to my email. A week later I auditioned for the role and after several callbacks over the next two months, I was offered a significant role in the series. You can call it courage, or audacity. I call it exploiting a window of opportunity.

☑

I returned to my reserves of courage once again in the midst of my private *The List* journey. I arrived in New York for work and remembered that Oprah (one of the items in my list) had offices in the city.

I went to a bookstore and purchased her magazine. At the bottom of the first page was the address of her offices and in one of the following pages was a list of all the employees, starting with the editorial assistant and all the way up to **Gayle King**, the Editor-In-Chief and Oprah's good friend.

I sat myself down to write a personal letter to Oprah, telling her my story, about the blog's journey, *The List*, and my desire to meet her in order to thank her for her positive influence on me during my teenage years. I made a copy of the letter for each of her employees and wrote: "Please give to Oprah." I stuffed them into envelopes and drove to the magazine's headquarters on 57th Street in Manhattan.

A security guard greeted me when I entered the building.

"Where are you headed?" he asked.

"I'm headed to Oprah's offices. I have invitations here for the Fox summer party," I answered. Yes, I lied. But you must admit, I did it gracefully and with originality. He directed to me Oprah's mailroom a few floors up.

One of her employees took the envelopes from me. "These are very important letters," I explained to her. "I must make sure they get to their addressees." "Don't worry," she answered and pointed to their mailboxes. That was enough for me. I left the building a few minutes later.

I have not heard from Oprah's people yet, but there is no doubt in my mind that out of the 100 people I sent my letter to, at least one will choose to help me and pass on my message. Why have I not heard from her yet? I don't know, but that will most certainly be one of the first questions I will ask her when we meet.

I know it's just a matter of time until it happens. I don't wait for the universe to hear me—I make every effort and take all the steps that I can to realize my dreams. Even if some of the steps eventually turn out to be wrong or excessive. I have learned to hone my messages and express them appropriately in order to achieve my goals.

I HAVE LEARNED TO BROADCAST MY DREAMS WITH ENTHUSIASM. ENTHUSIASM IS CONTAGIOUS AND CAUSES PEOPLE TO IDENTIFY WITH THEM UNTIL THEY CAN'T REMAIN INDIFFERENT ANYMORE.

---

40 | WHERE WAS I WRONG ON THE WAY TO REALIZING MY DREAMS?

People who read the blog or listen to my lecture sometimes ask me: "Was everything you have done in life a success? Didn't you also receive some negative answers?"

The way was not always paved with rose petals. I've already told you that I don't have super powers. For every positive answer, whether professional or personal, and for every bit of help I have received, I had ten negative answers to show for it. I also had quite a few missed opportunities.

Whenever there is a conversation about self-fulfillment around me, I'm always surprised how easily people excuse their lack of initiative and blame it on luck. It's convenient to tell ourselves that we did not reach one goal or another because of luck.

We convince ourselves that others have better luck, or that they have better connections, or that they have a direct line to God. We ignore the fact that we are fixated and that we have simply not taken the basic steps that could change our situation and move us forward.

Critics of *The List* love to tell me how lucky I am. How opening one door has led me to open another, which in turn has opened all the doors in the world for me. To answer them, I sat myself down and wrote a list (what else?) to prove that my achievements are simply a result of persistence, tenacity, and determination. Statistically, the more you try (and fail), the better your chances are of conquering your goals.

So for all of you who envy my luck, here is my list of unlucky situations in my life:

✔ **My parents divorced each other when I was eight years old.**

✔ **At the age of sixteen, I had an accident that left me wheelchair-bound for two years.**

✔ **I do not have a high school diploma.**

✔ **My brain consistently refuses to learn multiplication tables.**

✔ It also refuses to learn the alphabet.

✔ I have been cheated twice.

✔ I had money stolen from me twice, once by my partner.

✔ I have taken out some very stupid and unnecessary loans.

✔ I have been lied to.

✔ I am prone to being overweight.

✔ I had a TV talk show that was canceled before I even started filming.

✔ At least twelve people I trust have gravely disappointed me.

✔ A TV show, which I was working on, was canceled after only three months.

✔ I heard the words "No thanks" on 278 dates.

✔ I heard the words "No thanks" after 648 auditions.

✔ The producer of a play I worked on for two months declared bankruptcy and the play was canceled.

✔ I have been lied to. I know I have written this already, but it's happened so many times.

✔ My house has been burgled and everything has been stolen, including my daughter's diapers, frozen meatballs from the fridge, and a used toothbrush.

✔ During our attempts to have another child, we had several miscarriages.

Do you still think I'm luckier than others? Do you still think that God is always on my side?

Please don't answer. Let me . . . I work really hard to achieve what I want to and realize my dreams. Furthermore, anyone can work hard to shape their reality and, in many cases, change it. People think that success falls on you from the sky, gift-wrapped, with a big bow. People don't stop to think how much they need to sacrifice, give up, dare, and fight in order to make their dreams come true. Those who are afraid to take that first step don't know how many disappointments still lie ahead.

We all have traumas that we carry. Despite becoming adults, deep down we all feel like ugly ducklings. There are those who choose to let that burden paralyze them but then there are some who get rid of the dead weight somewhere over the sea and fly up toward their dreams. And in case you were wondering, it is a matter of choice which group you belong to.

Sometimes it just seems like success is something you pluck from a tree, but in fact success is something you have to sow. So every time you come across success, you should know that it's not coincidental. Remember that someone has worked very hard and sweated (even in air-conditioned spaces) just to make it grow and bloom for a long time.

So what is my secret? I don't linger on the negative, and choose to be happy about the positive.

☑

I do not have the best of relationships with math, but I'm a big believer in statistics. At any given moment in my career, when I wanted to get ahead, I sent dozens and sometimes hundreds of emails, offering my professional services. Two or three places always replied, inviting me to a meeting or an interview. There is always someone vacating a job, or going on maternity leave, and this is not the kind of information that's published in the job ads.

This is how I operate in my personal life too. When I was looking for the love of my life, I decided that I was taking on a dating "job." At the height of my "finding love project," I had a date every single day. It was pretty exhausting (but also amusing) and eventually it paid off. I learned what I was looking for and I learned what to say and what not to say on dates. Statistics, as always, were in my favor.

THERE WERE MISTAKES. NOT EVERYTHING I TRIED SUCCEEDED, AND NOT EVERY ACT OR DREAM I ATTEMPTED MOVED ME FORWARD. THERE WERE WHAT YOU WOULD PROBABLY CALL "FAILURES." I CHOOSE TO REGARD THEM AS LESSONS AND NOT AS DEFEATS.

During the first six months of the blog's existence, I worked hard on achieving my goals. I answered each and every email and sent messages to people I thought could help me. I worked to promote my blog on social networks and even invested money in promoting some of my statuses to get more buzz. My experience tells me that every dollar spent on public relations, marketing, and Internet promotions has paid back four-fold. I met with people who in turn connected me to others, I did interviews, and I uploaded hundreds of lists. I gave lectures for free, just to create a buzz around the project.

Surprisingly it was the "Australia" item on my list, which seemed the hardest at first, that was moving with greatest speed. I had scheduled the flight in my calendar, but eventually personal circumstances, the two miscarriages that we had while trying to conceive our second daughter, prevented my trip.

Things were moving and then got stuck. Pretty quickly, I found myself drained of energy and exhausted. Long hours of my day were dedicated to corresponding with people around the world, chasing my dreams.

I made quite a few mistakes on the way. One of them—or rather a few of them—were related to the Oprah item on my list. In addition to the letters I had left for her in New York, I filmed a series of funny short films, which I uploaded onto YouTube. At the end of each film, a narrator announced: "Yuval Abramovitz and Oprah Winfrey—a love story, coming soon on your TV screen!"

I found the email addresses of the producers on Oprah's team and sent them the links to the films. I also tweeted the films and sent them to the producers' Facebook pages. I was being excessive. I guess you could say I lost perspective.

One of the gossip reporters mocked me in an article: "Yuval Abramovitz is harassing Hollywood." At the time I was angry with him, but he was right.

Today, I understand that my behavior came across like an obsessed stalker. I assume that in light of the pressure I placed on them, there may well now be a picture hanging on the hallways of Oprah's office with my name and the caption: "BEWARE! CRAZY FAN!"

I began to understand that some of my messages were not focused, and this is why it was hard for me to realize them.

Unlike the Woody Allen fan who succeeded in meeting him by intriguing him with her academic research, I did not explain to Oprah how *The List* relates to the values of self-fulfillment that she promotes every day to her millions of followers. I was busy telling her about how I used to be paralyzed and how I wanted to close the circle and meet her. I may have conveyed weakness or a sense of entitlement instead of strength.

I didn't share with her my list-based television series idea (one of the items in my original list). This is something that might have interested her, not just personally, but also professionally. If I had shared a personal interest in meeting Oprah, maybe she would have developed a professional interest in meeting me and hearing about a show that might have been a good fit for the programming schedules of her television channel.

Every once in a while I wonder what Oprah's staff must have thought, being bombarded with my unfocused messages in their inboxes, on their personal Facebook pages, mail boxes, and on Twitter.

I HAVE MADE QUITE A FEW MISTAKES ON MY WAY TO SELF-FULFILLMENT. I DIDN'T MANAGE MY SCHEDULE CORRECTLY, I BOMBARDED PEOPLE WITH EMAILS IN A WAY THAT WAS BORDERLINE HARASSMENT, AND I DIDN'T EXPRESS MYSELF SUCCINCTLY ON MANY OCCASIONS. I HAVE MADE MANY MISTAKES, AND IN THE NEXT CHAPTERS I WILL INTRODUCE YOU TO WAYS THAT WILL SPARE YOU THE SAME AGGRAVATION IN EXECUTING YOUR LISTS.

---

41 | BE AUDACIOUS AND INSOLENT
BUT IN MODERATION

If your list includes items that involve people from other countries, remember that their mentality, etiquette, and codes of behavior may differ from yours. What you perceive as humor may be offensive to others. Your campaign can be as audacious as you like, as long as you don't go overboard, like I did during my attempts to meet Oprah.

People I don't know often contact me on Facebook asking for my advice, or just looking for my professional opinion.

I make sure I always reply to those who have a clear message, and find myself ignoring those who write random, pointless messages such as "When you are here, let me know!" "Is it really you?" "Are you there?"

How do I reply to these kinds of questions? Yes, it's me?

THERE IS NO SECOND CHANCE FOR A FIRST IMPRESSION.
MAKE SURE YOUR MESSAGE IS
ALWAYS REASONED AND ACCURATE.

The line between audacity and harassment is thin and being insolent might close doors for you. Make sure you focus your appeals and tailor them to suit the people you turn to for help. Mention why reaching your goal is important, what your interest is, and how they can benefit from helping you.

An interest is not a crude word. Benefitting our helpers (even mentally) can definitely accelerate the process. Make sure you are always ready to go, in case you happen to meet people who can help your cause.

Every once in a while I get remarks like: "These kinds of things only happen to you." And: "How does this always happen for you?"

It happens for one reason. My eyes are always wide open and my ears are always attuned to what is happening around me. I facilitate opportunities and I try hard not to miss them. I make sure I identify people who can assist me. Many times I have encountered closed doors, but instead of despairing or taking offense, I open an alternative door, or try to enter through the window by sending an email, a tweet, or a private message on Facebook.

During the 400 days campaign, I traveled the world with a business card that had an intentionally vague sentence printed on it: "I only have 400 days, please help me." Under the sentence was a link and a QR code leading to the blog. Thanks to the business card, many people have visited the blog and posted their lists on it. I also asked my friends to help me spread the message.

One morning I woke up and realized that *The List* had taken over my life.

42 | WANTED: A TIME ACCOUNT MANAGER AND CLEAR PHRASING

The details of my daily schedule, my fields of work, my lifestyle, my family, and my hobbies have all been described in previous chapters. So that I could manage all of these things successfully, and using the concept that time is money, I needed a considerably large "time account." As *The List* was getting more popular, my "time account" was sending out "time checks," left right and center. In other words, I was handing out time I didn't have.

The reckless spender of that time was called *The List*. To put it mildly, *The List* took over all of my free time, threatened my relationships with my relatives and colleagues, and of course started to interfere with other professional projects.

I needed a plan to manage my time.

Firstly, I decided to only spend two hours a day working on *The List*. I split the workload into two main tasks, managing the blog and answering emails, and allocated a maximum of fifteen minutes to each task.

During the first few days, I was quite generous with myself and didn't keep an eye on the time. Even when I was a bit stricter, I still noticed that I was exceeding the allotted time. So I decided to take action. I put a timer near my computer that would brutally cut off any task that took more than the designated fifteen minutes. Once it beeped, I had to move onto the next task, regardless of whether I had finished it. That was the only way I could move forward without drowning in my "to do" list.

Do you really need a beeping timer and such strict rules? Not necessarily. Looking back, the wasted time was simply a result of poor planning.

This is where I invite you to learn from my own experience how *not* to phrase your list. Sometimes knowing what not to do is every bit as important as understanding what you need to do.

WHAT NOT TO DO WHEN PHRASING AN EFFECTIVE LIST.

Do not cut corners.

We need to accurately phrase our aspirations out of an honest intention and a real desire to achieve them.

What do I mean?

In the list that started my experiment, I wrote that I wanted a toned, six-pack tummy. How does someone with a sweet tooth, who hates gyms, write such an unfocused item on his list? It's only good for a person who is completely unaware of their own limitations or who has infinite time—and who does? Where is that six-pack tummy supposed to come from? By being sculpted by a wicked plastic surgeon?

Today, I can honestly say that I didn't really care about having a six-pack tummy.

I wrote it because I knew it would draw enough visitors and media attention to my blog, and it did.

Don't get me wrong. I don't object to being slimmer, but it would have been better if I had set myself a more focused and realistic goal. One that encouraged me to start exercising right away, rather than a big task that demands complete devotion, a change of habits, and a complete genetic makeover.

Another unfocused item on my list involved going back to study and completing my high school diploma. If you're a thirty-seven-year-old with a relatively flourishing career, what the hell is going to make you dive back into Pythagoras' Theorem or quadratic equations? Why the hell did I think I would have enough drive and motivation to go back and finish my high school studies when my career doesn't seem to care if I have that particular qualification?

And if I had so badly misphrased these two items, how would I be able to sell *The List* as a TV show when my own list still needed focusing and readjustments?

I wrote myself a challenging list of goals, but forgot to think about how I was planning to achieve them. I was throwing darts everywhere without aiming them at a clear target.

So having broken down the process I went through to write the book you are now holding, it'd be fair to say that there was at least one stage along the way in which I found myself looking in the mirror realizing I had absolutely no clue.

No clue how to write lists that really work. No clue how to articulate goals and achieve them. No clue how to turn theory into practice, since everything I wrote in my own list was an intuitive, subconscious stream of youthful mischief, naïve dreams, and mere fantasies.

Despite the sharp pain that it caused me, it was undoubtedly a defining moment, a real breakthrough leading to an epiphany about how an efficient list should be written. I had discovered a tactic that enabled me to create a clear framework, one I felt I could put my name on and pass on to those who chose to invest time and money in this book. It laid down the infrastructure required to realize those dreams, and has proved helpful for myself. I hope you will find it helpful too.

A REVELATION: A LIST OF DREAMS IS NOTHING LIKE A GROCERY LIST.

As I read the lists that were sent to me (more than 5,000, from all around the world) and heard the lists that were written during my lectures and workshops, I started recognizing the patterns that created obstacles and prevented writers from realizing their aspirations, which meant that many would be giving up on their dreams long before they reached their goal.

Please go back to your list of 100 dreams for a moment and read it again thoroughly. Are there commonalities in the phrasing of the different items?

We all write in our lists general objectives that we aspire to achieve, such as:

- ☐ Lose weight
- ☐ Have a house with a swimming pool
- ☐ Meet Donald Trump
- ☐ Publish a book
- ☐ Open a café

While these are all beautiful, worthy dreams, the obstacle to realizing them is in the phrasing, which focuses on the bottom line, the final result. We give a name to our dream, but have no idea how to reach it. Even if we hang it on a pillar in the middle of our living room, it will not advance us toward knowing how to achieve it.

Even though I have read many lists, I hardly ever encounter one that has been phrased as a list of baby steps. I made the exact same mistake with my initial list.

Have a six-pack.

That's great, Yuval. But how are you going to have a six-pack if you don't like exercising? How are you going to be slim if you love pizza and ice cream so much?

That is when I had a revelation. I had to perfect my list and make it more accurate but mostly break it down into little steps, little manageable goals.

LISTS SHOULD BE WRITTEN IN BABY STEPS.

When writing each and every item, I have to be aware of the steps I need to take me from where I am to where I want to be. Not jump ahead without having a clear road to take me there.

So instead of writing: "Get a six-pack," I should write: "Find a physical activity I can sustain and as a result I will shape up and maybe eventually have a six-pack." The desired result is the final rung of a tall ladder but there are many small, sweaty baby steps on the way up there.

As soon as I understood that, I began searching for a physical activity I felt comfortable with. I tried yoga, Pilates, biking, and spinning. I enjoyed myself and suffered at the same time, but the results and the compliments were quick to follow. Eventually, I realized that considering my hectic life and my fear of going to a gym full of fit, muscular people wearing tight pants, I should probably find a less public solution. So, in spite of all the warnings about treadmills being an expensive clothes hanger, I purchased myself a handsome athletic treadmill. And lo and behold, this solution is working for me.

I ceremoniously placed the treadmill in our bedroom and found a few minutes at the beginning and at the end of every day to climb on it and run to nowhere. While I'm there, I catch up on television shows and movies and my "time accountant" is very happy about my multi-tasking. Subsequently I have discovered the joys of swimming and I make sure I swim three times a week.

How much closer am I to crossing off that specific item on my list? Thanks to the treadmill and swimming, I have already dropped eleven pounds. I'm still not there, but if I'm consistent, maybe I'll eventually have one can out of the six. And if not, I will still feel satisfied with my fit body.

☑

The owner of a website called me and asked to interview me about *The List*.

"As 'Mr. Lists' I have to ask you a question. I'm thirty-nine years old and I only have one dream. To find a supporting, loving life partner. How do you suggest I realize this dream?"

"Do you date a lot?" I asked. "I mean, do you actually treat it like a job?"

"Not really." She flinched. "Dating is a nightmare."

"But you do understand that dating is the most common way to form a connection? Do you have a profile on a dating website?"

"No! I can't stand the idea."

"What about speed dating? I hear from friends that it's great fun."

"No way. It's not for me."

"What about a matchmaking agency?"

"Oh God no!" She was horrified.

"I have an idea." I smiled. "Throw a dinner party at your house, invite friends, and ask each guest to bring one single man. Kind of a potluck party, but instead of pies and quiches, people bring men . . ."

She laughed. She liked the idea.

"Do you know what your next goal should be? Not 'finding a husband' but 'finding pleasant ways to meet eligible men.' Once you find a way of dating that suits you, go on a least one date a week and you will eventually reach your final goal, which is to find a husband."

43 | THE CHALLENGE:
WEIGHING YOUR WORDS

Word your dream accurately. That was the advice I gave Neta, a friend of a friend, who shared with me her dream to open a nursery school. For two years she had been speaking her dream aloud, but couldn't manifest it. A short conversation with her revealed that it takes about $30,000 to start such a school, and she didn't have a cent to put toward it.

"In that case," I told her, "you need to rewrite your dream. The phrasing should be: 'I'm finding a way to raise money to establish a nursery school.'"

I told Neta about the many funds whose purpose it is to encourage and support small businesses, as well the easy-to-get loans that the banks were offering. Another option I thought she could look into was having an investor-partner. Neta started exploring all of these suggestions at the same time, and within two months she received a development grant for the whole amount from just one of the funds. Today her school is celebrating its second year; it is working to its full capacity and is receiving warm recommendations from the neighborhood's parents.

It's a good time to admit that I knew your list of 100 dreams wasn't going to be all that focused. My list wasn't either in the beginning. However, it is important to me to take you through the whole grueling journey of writing a huge list so you can be really aware of the bumps you are going to have to overcome on your way to your final list by the end of this book.

Try to not only accurately phrase your dreams, but also find the quickest paths that will lead you to realizing them. Each dream has more than one path leading to it and you must find the one that will be the most effective for you.

When you compose a list, don't use words that cannot be easily defined. What does it mean to be "fulfilled, "successful," or "happy"? These terms are very elusive.

Let's say I publish a book and sell a thousand copies. Have I succeeded or failed? From my point of view, the mere manifestation of an imagined story into a book is already a success, not to mention selling 1000 copies. From my publisher's point of view, for whom success is sales, it is a failure, since their investment will not yield much in the way of profit.

And what does it mean to "be rich"? Is someone who owns a house and a fancy car rich? Does earning 200,000K per annum make someone rich? Or perhaps it is someone who simply can afford the life they want, and someone who takes pleasure in life within the boundaries of common sense? Being rich is not just a matter of money, but also a state of mind.

So, when you compose your list, define exactly what you want. Not "to be rich," but "to earn enough money to save for retirement or go on vacation when I feel like it."

ONLY WHEN I REALIZED HOW IMPORTANT IT WAS TO PROPERLY ARTICULATE MY GOALS ON THE WAY TO ACHIEVING THEM DID I GET CLOSER TO PERFORMING MY TASKS QUICKLY AND MORE EFFECTIVELY. IT WAS THE BABY STEPS THAT HELPED ME ADVANCE FASTER TOWARD THE GOAL.

The following exercise is intended to help you clarify and sharpen your phrasing. I will put two identical lists in front of you, differently phrased. Decide which one you think is more effective.

LIST NUMBER 1:

- ☐ Find love.
- ☐ Drop twenty pounds.
- ☐ Travel in South America for two months.
- ☐ Document Grandma and Grandpa's life story.
- ☐ Be a famous fashion designer.
- ☐ Meet Martha Stewart.
- ☐ Redecorate my bedroom.
- ☐ Organize a high school reunion for my class.
- ☐ Purchase a giant flat screen TV.
- ☐ Learn to sculpt.

LIST NUMBER 2:

- [ ] Go on at least two dates a week to increase my chances of finding love.

- [ ] Give up sugar (I'm a sweet tooth remember!). Join a support group and jog at least two times a week, in order to lose twenty pounds within the next six months.

- [ ] Talk to my boss about the possibility of taking a leave of absence for two months and go on a two-month trip through South America.

- [ ] Schedule a meeting with Grandma and Grandpa this week, and three more later on, to interview them and document their life story.

- [ ] Take the time to thoroughly research design schools and sign up for next round of admissions.

- [ ] On the way back from South America, stop in New York and sit in the audience of the Martha Stewart show and maybe try to meet her personally.

- [ ] Take $2000 out of my saving account to paint my bedroom, install shelves, and change the light fixture and the curtains.

- [ ] Open a Facebook group called "Class of 97—Alonim School" and invite all my high school friends (where the hell is my yearbook?!) to join. Then suggest a reunion.

- [ ] Start saving $100 a month toward purchasing a TV by the end of the year.

- [ ] Ask about sculpting courses around my area and go to a trial lesson.

As you can see, both lists ultimately contain the same goals, but only one focuses on the ways of achieving them. From the moment I understood that writing a list of "super objectives" was just inefficient, I started to rethink all the lists I had written in the past. It demanded more time and effort, but it paid off. My lists became more focused and effective because I could see the path to achieving them right in front of me. The path was practically paved for me.

44 | NARROWING YOUR LIST

Let's get back to your list of 100 dreams.

Now that you understand how important it is to accurately formulate your goals, it's time to review and refine your list.

Go get your personal list notebook—you've got work to do!

Clear some time. Sit down to process, narrow down, and accurately rephrase every item. Refine your list, put some work into it, and eventually it will work for you.

If we take my basic assumption that fondness for chocolate can't help me with my six-pack item, maybe it means that it's time to put a item in my list that says: "keep my home sugar-free."

The first step in narrowing down your list is erasing items that are not very feasible. It's important to understand that the term "feasible" is relative. You need to examine how feasible a goal is to you, in accordance with your abilities.

Let's say you wrote "act in a Hollywood movie" or "win an Oscar." You need to ask yourself: "Have I ever acted before? Am I a professional actor? Do I have a convincing American accent?" If you answered "yes" to those questions, that goal is feasible for you. If the peak of your acting career was acting in a school play in third grade, then it is not a realistic goal.

Having examined the feasibility of the item, do you still want to get to Hollywood? Great! Sign up for an acting course first thing in the morning. Then go register for an acting school for the next semester. That is your immediate goal, since it's the first step toward your objective. Later on, you can set yourself a more advanced goal, like "act in a children's play," "audition for a commercial," "audition for a TV series." Work on your resume and eventually set "audition in Los Angeles" as a goal.

If Ayelet Zorer or Moran Atias, two successful Israeli actresses who relocated to the United States, wrote "Win an Oscar" on their lists, it would be realistic in relation to their talents and past achievements. Mind you they too have to break down their dream, for example: "Audition for movies that might be nominated for an Oscar."

In 2014, the Mexican-Kenyan actress, Lupita Nyong'o, a relatively unknown actress at the time, won an Oscar for her supporting role in the movie *12 Years a Slave*. Looking at her it may seem like everybody can win an Oscar—even a young, anonymous actress from Kenya.

While I do not claim that winning an Oscar is an achievement reserved only for Hollywood actors, if you take a glimpse at Nyong'o's biography, you'll see that long before the Oscar ceremony, she started her journey in acting schools both in Kenya and in the States. She also gained professional experience working on TV. And while it's true that her Oscar win was meteoric in terms of her short biography, she still had the experience that made her Oscar dream (common to most actors) a realistic dream.

Are you dreaming of owning your own house? Great. Write all the steps and goals that will lead you to your main objective in X number of years. For example: open a "house" savings account; take on another part-time job to increase your income and your savings; cut down monthly expenses by a certain amount. You could even move in with your parents for a period of time in order to save money that would otherwise go to rent. Learn how to invest in the stock market; ask that on your next birthday people bring cash instead of gifts.

If you do all of the above, you are likely to have enough money for a down payment that along with a reasonable mortgage will get you your dream house.

After having refined your list and having narrowed it down to "realistic" and "non-realistic" (in relation to your life's circumstances), it's time for another narrowing—according to how much you want things. Break it apart and focus on what you really want to do, then what you want to do, but not right now.

For example, if you wrote "volunteer" (for any good cause), but you only wrote it because it sounded good, and you don't really have the time and don't see yourself doing it any time soon, give up that item. The list should be accurate and its items should be derived from true passion and dedication to realizing them. Be honest and make sure to write only the things you really and truly want. And the sooner the better.

AIM HIGH, BUT AIM REALISTICALLY!

45 | THE LIVES
OF OTHERS

DID YOU GET IN TOUCH WITH YOUR REALISTIC SIDE? WERE YOU VERY HONEST AND ACCURATE? DID YOU REFINE AND FOCUS?

Wonderful. Now go back to your list and clean out the dreams and goals that are not relevant to you, the ones you can't control. This is a very significant process.

In my lectures and workshops, I often come across items that people write in regards to other people: "Marry off my son," "Encourage my husband to go for the promotion," "Get my parents to stop fighting" or "Have my daughter enroll herself in a good university."

These kinds of things are not up to us to achieve even if we try really hard. It's up to the person in question to take the necessary steps to achieve those goals. We can be there for that person, show them the way, and help guide them toward the path we have recommended, but we cannot force them to do so.

I recently received an email from a man who had attended my lecture:

"Yuval, do you think that a list of dreams is able to solve or change personal conflicts with spouses, siblings, parents, children, or any other close person? And if so, how would you do it? How exactly would you phrase it in your list?"

"That's an excellent question," I answered, "and I can tell you one thing I have learned in my journey: You can't control other people's dreams, no matter how close they are to you. Let's say you have a daughter, a thirty-year-old bachelorette, and on your list you write: 'To marry off my daughter.' Between the two of us, your daughter will get married when she finds the right person and wants to marry. You, as her father, cannot control her will and her actions. You can only control how you feel about what she does. Therefore, your list should focus on how you intend to handle the situation. For example: 'Ignore intrusive questions from aunts about our single daughter,' 'Ask family members not to bring up the sensitive subject during dinner,' and so on."

"That's what I thought." I could practically hear his disappointment in his email. "So how do you deal with a situation that has to do with a close family member who you can't change or accept? How do you live with a situation, a character, or a trait that drives you increasingly mad?"

"You set a new goal," I answered. "'To not get annoyed by what isn't in my control.'"

Mutual goals that involve spouses or family members require matching expectations and dreams. I once met a couple, where the wife was convinced that their joint bank account was like a suitcase full of money, while the husband . . . to put it mildly . . . did not share her feeling.

They were one economic entity, but while the wife had recklessly spent money, the husband had worked very hard in order to increase the family income. Had they worked together on a mutual list of goals, they could have saved themselves a lot of time and frustration.

WE DON'T HAVE CONTROL OVER THE CHOICES OF OTHER PEOPLE, NO MATTER HOW CLOSE TO US THEY MAY BE. IF WE INCLUDE ITEMS IN OUR LIST THAT REGARD THE LIVES OF OTHERS, WE'RE ONLY LOOKING TO FOR DISSAPPOINTMENT.

That's a lesson I've learned from experience. As you may recall, in my original list I had a item: "Try to rehabilitate a homeless person," resulting from the disappointment I felt after having tried, two years prior, to do just that.

It was the summer I had my list published, and I was wandering the steaming city for days on end trying to find a homeless person I could communicate with. Eventually, and with the encouragement of a local TV crew that was filming an article about The List, I found a homeless person who wanted to leave the streets.

I set up an appointment to meet with him at an agreed-upon spot on Allenby Street in Tel Aviv. I bought him breakfast and listened to his story while he was devouring the food. He told me about how he had been thrown out of his home, began associating with the wrong people, got addicted to alcohol and drugs, and found himself on the street.

His story touched me, and the hope for his rehabilitation seemed closer than ever before. Again and again I imagined, with satisfaction, how I would help him reclaim his life and find a job, how he would finally have a warm bed, shower, and clean clothes. We set to meet a few days later, but he never showed up. I looked for him all over town, but couldn't find him—not even where he used to sit before. It was the second time I wanted to help a homeless person, but he disappeared as if he'd never existed.

This is when I understood that my will to help another person cannot materialize unless the other side is equally interested. After a few more failed attempts to locate a homeless person to rehabilitate, I decided to give up that item in my original list and focus on other things over which I have control and the power to change something.

GOD,
GRANT ME THE SERENITY
TO ACCEPT THE THINGS I CANNOT CHANGE,
THE COURAGE TO CHANGE THE THINGS I CAN,
AND THE WISDOM TO KNOW THE DIFFERENCE.

(Serenity Prayer)

46 | WHAT'S THE SCORE?

I'm frequently asked: "How many goals can I achieve in one year?"

There isn't one answer that will fit everybody. The number of goals you will achieve depends on your energy, true desire to achieve them, the amount of free time you have on your hands, and of course the size of your dreams and the number of baby steps that it will take to achieve them.

AND YET, HOW MANY ITEMS SHOULD YOU INCLUDE IN YOUR LIST?

In my opinion and for the sake of practicality, it's best to work with ten goals, in a time frame of two years.

Why two years? Because in that time frame we can see the horizon and still keep positive energy for doing and achieving.

Goals to be achieved in ten years are too distant. The path may be so long, impossible, and frustrating that we end up giving up on our goal.

This is why you have to find ways to keep your mental strength and try not to make things too hard for yourself.

I have heard the opposite approach, which claims that it's better to set a lot of goals and dreams and to work toward all of them at the same time, while on the other hand, I've heard many times that our energy is limited and expandable, as is our time.

Now try to look at things from another point of view.

WHEN YOU DO, YOU REALIZE

WHEN YOU REALIZE, YOU ARE HAPPY AND PLEASED

WHEN YOU ARE HAPPY AND PLEASED, YOU FILL UP WITH ENERGY

WHEN YOU FILL UP WITH ENERGY, YOU ACT QUICKLY AND PASSIONATELY

WHEN YOU ACT QUICKLY AND PASSIONATELY, YOU DO MORE IN A SHORTER TIME

In recent years, I have had the privilege of having many one-on-one intimate conversations with successful people around the world, all of whom have thriving careers and big families with many children.

One of the most successful authors I've met is Smadar Shir, a mother of six children, who publishes more than one book a year and still has time to write articles for newspapers, give lectures, and volunteer. When I asked her how she finds the time for everything, her simple answer, which may annoy or frustrate you, was: "The bigger my load is, the more focused I am."

A similar answer was given to me again and again by a many active and successful people. A load of tasks commits us to immediate action, raising energy and enthusiasm.

Our performance and successes generate more energy in us for doing and acting and every success becomes another layer in our sense of capability and ability to realize our dreams.

EVERY SUCCESS LEADS TO ANOTHER SUCCESS. THIS IS NOT A VICIOUS CYCLE! IT'S AN ELECTRIC CIRCUIT OF ENTHUSIASM, AND IT ALWAYS WORKS—I GUARANTEE IT.

In sports medicine it is well known that those who arrive to practice refreshed will gain more from the exercise than those who arrive tired and spent. So is the case with sporting events: Upright and energetic competitors are often those who take the podium.

Make sure you transmit enthusiasm and faith in your dream. If you don't believe in yourself and your dream, how can you expect others to?

Many ask me, does achieving goals guarantee happiness?

Words like "happiness" or "success" are personal, cannot be objectively defined, and are also temporary by nature.

My lists have not made me immune to heartache, but they have certainly improved my sense of personal happiness and made the people around me happier, at least about anything regarding their interaction with me.

Once you finish narrowing your list of 100 dreams down into one conclusive list, you will have no more than ten realistic dreams. Write a tentative deadline next to each goal. This will not be an accurate date set in stone, but an estimate: In three months, in the summer, or by the end of next year.

NOW IS THE TIME TO ACT!

47 | HOW DO WE START REALIZING OUR LIST?

Go through the items of your list. Let's start realizing!

Choose the goal that makes your pulse quicken, the one that is your biggest passion. It is the one you must, really must, start realizing, right now, before all others.

Yes, **NOW** is the key word.

Be on your way now. No putting it off for later, no excuses.

Start realizing your goal once you finish reading this line. Get the process going and take the first step toward the goal.

Gradually, take one more step, and then another one on the way toward ticking that goal off the list. Then add another achievable goal, then another one.

The fact that you set yourself a few goals is not supposed to prevent you from trying to achieve all of them at the same time. You never know which seed will sprout first and grow the fastest. This is why you should sow and water your entire flowerbed at the same time. In the next spring, or the one after it, you will have a blooming garden.

This may be the place to specify that the word "dreams" is not meant only in regard to high and mighty aspirations, like conquering a mountain top, or meeting an idolized star, but also in regard to little tasks, wills, and goals, which gnaw at our mind continuously and prevent us from making our way to new ones.

One of my small and very realistic dreams (which I share with many people) is to organize the thousands of pictures on my phone, download them to my computer, sort them and organize them in folders, print the best ones, and put them in a scrapbook. Technological advancement has turned all of us into semi-professional photographers, but most of us do not keep the photos we take. This mundane task can be done within three days at the most. One day to sort them into folders, one to print, and another to organize them in a scrapbook. So where's the problem?

I bet you all have one small goal that you have been putting off. Maybe you have a few digital notes on your phone, containing many different tasks. Why don't you declare them your immediate goals? I saw many little dreams people wrote, like learning to ride a bike, reconciling with an estranged grandmother, fixing their front teeth, treating an ingrown toenail, arranging their closet, emptying their garage, and little things that may seem like a nightmare, but living with the guilt and dissatisfaction that lies in postponing those tasks is the bigger tragedy.

SURROUND YOURSELF WITH YOUR LIST.

Now you only have two more stages left.

When you have a final list, make copies of it and post them in as many places around you as possible, so that you have a constant reminder of your dreams. Put one copy under your pillow or next to your bed, hang one on your refrigerator, one next to your calendar, one in your bag, and one in the car.

Someone who attended my lecture said she was going to put one copy of her list on her computer desktop so that she sees it every time she sits down to work or surf the web. Then she tried to be more accurate and said, "On second thoughts, it's going to be a problem since everyone will be able to see what I wrote."

"And what's the problem with that?" I wondered.

"My list is private and only meant for my eyes," she recited the most common excuse, which in my opinion is wrong.

"The only things that maybe you should perhaps be hide are items such as 'finding a lover to replace my husband,'" I answered her.

She laughed. Her husband, who was sitting next to her, didn't find it as funny.

48 | NEEDED: A DISTRIBUTOR

We have now reached the final and most important part of preparing a list: distributing it and sharing it with the world.

DREAMS ARE NOT MEANT
TO BE WHISPERED IN THE DARK.
DREAMS ARE MEANT TO BLAZE UP LOUDLY.

I know that some of you are already accustomed to writing lists of goals, and I hope that the one new thing that I'm revealing to you, that maybe you didn't know, is understanding of the importance of publicity when it comes to these kinds of lists. This is the most important message of the book. Do not be content with a written list. Express it out loud. Enunciate it clearly and succinctly without shame or doubt.

Shout out your dreams to anyone who is willing to listen. Post them on social networks, publish them on your blog, talk to your friends about them and be the ambassador of your own goals, promote them. Make your lists public and don't hesitate to ask for help. The more people you share your list with, the more you increase your chances of realizing it. Statistics, remember?

Imagine yourself in a room full of thirty strangers. You stand on a platform and declare that your dream is opening a clothing store. There is a pretty good chance that at least one person in the room also wants to open such a store, or knows someone who is looking to invest or become a partner in such a business.

Now imagine the effect your speech would have if there were 100 people in the room. And what would happen if there were 500 people? How about 5,000?

YOU ARE THE BEST PROMOTER OF YOUR OWN DREAMS!

In the middle of my lecture I invite everybody to use the pens in front of them and write lists, just like you did while working with this book.

I give the participants a few minutes to refine and accurately describe their dreams, and then I ask each person to read two items out loud and commit himself or herself, in front of everybody else, to acting towards realizing one of the two. At almost every lecture, magic happens. People dare to share their dreams, and almost always they receive initial help from the other people in the room.

The more people in the room, the more tips and solutions arise, which help the dreamers take the first steps toward realizing and achieving. The energy that spreads throughout the room and is felt by everybody is amazing. Once the first few brave souls open their hearts, share their dreams, and expose their lists, it takes no more than a few minutes for the others to break the ice and start helping them with information that will advance their goals. When I watch it from the platform, I feel uplifted and extremely excited.

In the last decade, we have become so accustomed to communicating with others through emails and social networks that we have forgotten how to talk to people.

HOWEVER, GOOD OLD FASHIONED FACE-TO-FACE COMMUNICATION HAS A GREAT POWER.

I particularly remember one lecture, in which everyone who attended had benefited from substantial help of others in the room. One woman admitted that she had never ridden a bike and that, at the age of forty, she feared it would never happen. Someone in the audience immediately offered to teach her how to ride. Another said she dreamed about investing in the stock market and a business consultant offered his services. Since she couldn't afford it, she offered to barter; she would teach him how to lose weight (she was a coach for addiction rehabilitation) and he would teach her how to invest in the stock market.

In another lecture, there was a woman whose dream was to design and construct a building, as a part of a business plan. She was immediately swooped up by a real estate entrepreneur, an architect, a businessman's wife who had mentioned how her husband was looking for projects to invest in, and people in the audience who wanted to buy or rent an apartment.

"I think we just formed a purchase group," I laughed. None of the people in the room had known anyone else in the room before or known what they did for a living, and here the magic worked again.

Someone else in the audience shared with the others—complete strangers—that his father, who had recently passed away, had left him and his brother a plot of land in the north of the country.

"My dream is to build a little villa there and rent it out but there's no way I can do that. It requires an investment of at least two million dollars," he said with sadness in his eyes.

"It really doesn't," one of the others in the room enlightened him. "My family has had a villa for a few years now, and they only invested about $150,000 to build it."

"My husband is a business consultant," revealed someone else. "I'm sure he'd love to meet with you and build a business plan for free."

I recommended a website that tries to connect business partners to one another, and promised to hook him up with my very nice banker (I make sure to empower those who empower me!) so she could examine loan options to help promote his dream.

At the end of the evening, the man had seven practical suggestions, a road map for action, and quite a few connections, all of it thanks to the fact that he had publicly announced his dream.

THINK OF THE ADVANTAGES THAT 21ST CENTURY TECHNOLOGY BESTOWS UPON US. AFTER ALL, BEFORE THE INTERNET AND SOCIAL NETWORKS, ALL WE COULD HAVE DONE WAS SHOUT OUR DREAMS THROUGH THE WINDOW AND HOPE THAT SOME NEIGHBOR WOULD HEAR. TODAY, ALL THE WINDOWS ARE OPEN FOR US TO BUILD A VIRTUAL BRIDGE FOR MILLIONS OF PEOPLE ALL AROUND THE WORLD TO HELP US TURN DREAMS INTO A REALITY.

49 | BEHAVIOR RULES FOR
THE DAY AFTER

A consolidated, focused, and well-articulated list is a significant step on the way to self-fulfillment, but now you have to take a deep breath. Rome wasn't built in a day, goes the cliché, and as clichés go, this one is true.

The way from a dream to reality is still long and bumpy, consisting of refusals, disappointments, and more downs than ups. This is why you need to keep breathing regularly, maintaining high levels of positive energy and strong faith. Not necessarily religious faith, but rather faith in yourself, your ability to move mountains and in the world around you, and the willingness of friends and strangers to help you.

At the same time, you must grow a thick skin and equip yourself with metaphoric ear plugs, because after you turn your list public, talk about it, and shout it out, for every person that will happily help, there will be at least three who will try to convince you it's a terrible idea.

We all know these types—the energy-sucking wing cutters. The bitter or just the plain jealous. Those who will always have something to say about your list, about your dreams, and especially about the naivete that makes you think you can reach your goals.

Along the way you will encounter people who will tell you that you are wasting your time on nonsense, suck your energy, dilute the oxygen in your blood, and load their paralyzing fears onto you, along with all the negative experiences they have accumulated in their lifetime.

50 | STAYING AWAY
FROM POISON

American author and therapist Dr. Lillian Glass, who wrote a great book called *Toxic People: 10 Ways of Dealing with People Who Make Your Life Miserable*, has met many patients who were surrounded by "toxic" people.

These people are not intentionally bad. They are often faithless, pessimistic people, who take the wind out of our sails because they don't know any better. They can be our bosses, our best friends, and even our children or spouses. We are surrounded by these people; sometimes we live with them or share a bed with them.

Toxic people will tell you, a second after you finish sharing your most intimate dream with them, that it is a stupid, redundant, dangerous idea, and that it has no potential and is a complete waste of time.

My beloved grandfather, for example, is a "toxic" person. He does not have an ounce of evil in him. Quite the contrary—he is a charming man and I owe much to him for the person I have become. My grandfather is a healthy and enthusiastic ninety-one-year-old man, full of life and up to date on everything that is going on. He watches popular TV shows and is able to have a lively discussion about the important matters of the day, the news headlines, and even a thing or two about reality TV shows.

My grandfather wants the best for me, and when we converse about my professional achievements he is never satisfied.

"How many students do you have in your writing school?" he asked me a few months after I had launched A Cultural Hero.

"Almost two hundred," I answered proudly.

"That's it? Why not more? Don't you work in the mornings and afternoons too?"

"Is that the whole amount you get upfront for your new book?" "Is that all of your annual profit from the store?" "Why did you only get five pages this week for your article and why wasn't your name on the cover?" "You didn't get enough air time this week."

I know he loves me very much and wants what is best for me. He thinks I deserve more and those comments are well intentioned and come from a loving place. However, the way he responds to me is still a negative influence on me, ruining my mood and lowering my energy.

At some point, I decided that I was better off keeping him out of certain aspects of my life, because otherwise, I wouldn't be able to maintain my high levels of energy and joy in what I do.

☑

In the last few years I have kept information from the faithless and sifted a lot of "toxic" people out of my life. I have distanced from me, and all those close to me, the energy suckers, the natural born pessimists, or those who have become toxic because life beat them. But whose life doesn't beat them every once in a while? Instead, I have tried to associate more with inspirational, successful people, whose eyes shine when they talk about the next step, the next business, the next dream. The multitaskers. Those who do a lot of things without caring about "what people will say." These are friends who I look up to in admiration, learn from, consult with, and know that their advice comes from an honest and loving place. I'm sure they want to see me successful and fulfilled and are not threatened or frustrated by someone else's success.

? | EXERCISE
CHECK YOURSELF:

Are you toxic to the dreams of the people around you? Or worse: are you toxic to your own dreams and ideas (no matter how big or small they may be)?

If you answered yes, it's time to get rid of that bad habit.

SURROUND YOURSELF WITH PEOPLE WHO ARE DREAMERS AND SUPPORTERS, THOSE WHO ARE BOLD, ENCOURAGING, AND INSPIRING.

WITH THEIR HELP YOU WILL FLY UP TO THE SKY AND EVEN HAVE A SPARE PARACHUTE IN CASE OF A FAILURE.

One of my writing students, Ravid Shavit, who heard about *The List* and Dr. Glass's theory of toxic people, shared a folk tale with me. It has a moral. Maybe you know it or one of its versions:

One morning, in a little village far, far away, a father woke up his young son and told him: "Rise and shine, child! Come with me to the big city and maybe you will learn something."

He took the donkey, lifted his son on to it, walked at its side, and they both went on their way.

When they walked through the gates of town, people looked at them and started saying: "Look at that ill-bred child! Instead of letting his elderly father ride the donkey, he lets him sweat in the sun." The father and son heard them talk, finished their business in the market, and went back to their village.

The next morning, the father woke up his son again and told him, "Rise and shine, child! Come with me to the big city and maybe you will learn something."

This time the father rode the donkey and the son walked by its side.

When they arrived in town, the town elders saw them and started talking: "What kind of a father is he, letting his young son walk and sitting on the donkey himself?" The father and son heard them talk, finished their errands in town, and went back to their village.

The next morning, once again, the father woke up his son and told him, "Rise and shine, child! Come with me to the big city and maybe you will learn something."

This time the two set on their way both riding on the donkey. In the town's gate they already had a group of people waiting to scold them: "Look at those two… don't they have a heart? A small, little donkey, already suffering from the heat, and they are both riding it. Are they trying to kill it?" The father and son heard them talk, finished their meeting with the pharmacist in town, and returned to their village.

The next morning, the father woke up his son and asked him to join him on his journey to town for the fourth time. This time, they both walked at the side of the donkey. The town's elders looked at them and started laughing hard: "Who is the donkey and who are the humans? They have a donkey and they are not riding it!" The father and son heard them talk, finished their meeting with the tailor in town, and returned to their village.

The next morning, the father woke up his son and sat down at his bed.

"Are we going to town today?" the son asked. "Am I going to learn something new today?"

"Every day we learn something new," said the father. "Understand, son, no matter what you do, or how you do it, there will always be those who will criticize you or mock your choices. You'd better live your life your own way, the way that suits you, the way that you want and love. Sometimes the result will be good and sometimes bad, but there will always be those who criticize you. Follow your heart and remember that I will always support you."

51 | WHY ARE YOU SO OBSESSIVE ABOUT **THOSE LISTS?**

I have often been asked where I derive my passion from when talking about lists and why those lists are so important to me.

When lecturing I ask people to set aside their cynicism and keep an open mind. Still, I'm asked over and over again, "But why even look for dreams to realize? Why not just live calmly and enjoy quiet evenings watching television?"

Well, I do not preach self-fulfillment at all costs, or a crazy headlong chase for dreams. In my opinion, there is a huge value in moderate idling, little joys, staring aimlessly or pondering. I can "waste" hours just napping, binge-watching DVDs, listening to music, or reading books. I don't see it as a waste of time; rather as a recharging of my batteries. Along with the time you allot to realizing the dreams in your list, make some time to enrich your inner self. That will refill your oxygen tank with renewed energy.

On the other hand, I believe that self-fulfillment strengthens our faith in ourselves. It creates a sense of value and self-confidence and stimulates our boldness to continuously set the bar higher for ourselves.

WHEN WE FEEL FULFILLED, ABLE, AND CAPABLE, OUR BRAIN RELEASES CHEMICALS THAT PROPEL US TO TRY AND RECREATE THE FEELING OF JOY THAT COMES FROM SUCCESS. THE SUCCESSES THAT ARE REGISTERED TO OUR NAME PUSH US FORWARD, TOWARD THE NEXT CHALLENGE. THEY ARE THE BUILDING BLOCKS OF OUR FUTURE DREAMS.

52 | HOW DO PEOPLE WRITE?

During The List lectures, I noticed a difference in the way people write their lists. I have learned to tell them apart. Here, for example, are three types of writers who sabotage their own dreams:

THE SCRIBBLERS—THOSE WHO DOUBTFULLY WRITE LITTLE LISTS OF FIVE OR SEVEN GOALS, AND DETERMINEDLY INSIST: "I HAVE NO OTHER DREAMS!"

THE SINNERS AGAINST THEMSELVES—THOSE WHO LET ME KNOW THAT IT'S NOT WORTHY FOR THEM TO INVEST SO MUCH ENERGY IN THE ATTEMPT TO REALIZE THEIR DREAMS, BECAUSE NO ONE PROMISES THEM SUCCESS.

SELF-POISONING—THOSE WHO CHOP THEIR OWN WINGS BEFORE THEY EVEN HAVE A CHANCE TO SPREAD THEM, AND DO NOT DARE TO TAKE OFF AND FLY. THEY MUMBLE: "I DON'T HAVE DREAMS," OR "THERE'S NO CHANCE THAT I WILL SUCCEED."

"I envy you for having so many dreams," a sixty-five-year-old woman emailed me, "because the more I think about it, I come to the conclusion that I don't have dreams at all. I have traveled the world and experienced a lot, fulfilled myself personally and professionally, I have children and grandchildren, and even enough money for my golden years."

And what about little dreams like meeting a friend for lunch, or taking your grandchild to the movies? How about reconciling with an old friend, or getting closer to your daughter who has grown distant lately?

Don't forget about the little dreams; they will provide you with some unforgettable moments.

The toxic type never stops surprising me with the amount of poison they inject into themselves. Not long ago, while writing this book, I sat with an old friend to talk about life. Naturally, the conversation turned to matters of The List and like many before her, she said to me, "Well, smarty, things come easy to you. Only people with high energy levels, like you, can fulfill themselves."

To the uninformed spectator, it may seem like I realize my dreams annoyingly easily when in fact, it's an illusion. I work very hard to reach my goals and dreams. There are days when I work sixteen hours and vacations I spend talking on the phone or working on the computer, because a window of opportunity that could bring me closer to my dream happened to open right then. Sometimes I get what I want, sometimes I don't, but because of my initial focus, and in respect to the number of goals I set for myself, the number of failures is relatively small.

Determining that I realize my dreams easily seems shallow to me, like determining that a conductor is merely a man waving his hands about.

It doesn't matter which profession you look at. A conductor, an acrobat, an actor, a makeup artist, a firefighter, a magician, an author, a playwright—it always looks like magic, as if they perform their jobs with no special effort and everything is easy for them because we don't witness the hours and hours of rehearsals and practice that they endure in order for the magic to appear seamless.

So how do I answer all those who think that it's Lady Luck that has been following me everywhere? To tell the truth, I don't see myself as an exceptionally lucky person. I've had a couple of "workplace accidents," as I've shared with you, but it never discouraged me. I have embraced my wise grandmother Sophia's words of wisdom: "When you wash dishes, you're bound to break some." In the same way, I believe that whoever shouts out his dreams in order to get help from others may sometimes get hurt along the way. However, I still trust everybody who approaches me. I'm willing to take the risk, in the hope of continuing to realize my dreams.

The right way is to do, do, do! Don't put your faith in Lady Luck, but in you and your willpower.

OUR FAITH AND OUR LUCK ARE IN OUR HANDS, AND THERE IS NOTHING THAT STANDS IN THE WAY OF WILL.

THE DETERMINED REWRITERS ARE ANOTHER GROUP OF LIST WRITERS I HAVE MET DURING MY LECTURES. AS OPPOSED TO THE DOUBTFUL SCRIBBLERS, WHO WRITE EVERYTHING CASUALLY AND SLOPPILY, THESE WRITERS FILL THREE OR FOUR PAGES WITH DOZENS OF ITEMS, REWRITE THEIR LIST AGAIN AND AGAIN, AND DO NOT PUT IT DOWN UNTIL THEY REACH A HIGH LEVEL OF ACCURACY.

These people usually have many realized dreams to their name. Naturally, some of them enjoy financial and social stability. It's interesting how it's the people who have realized things in their lives who let themselves continue to challenge themselves and their imagination, out of knowledge and faith that they can accomplish anything they want, and that an inventory of dreams is a living, breathing, and continuously updating organism.

There are many dreamers in our world whose success drives them forward to conquer more goals and broaden the boundaries of their knowledge and excitement.

☑

Richard Branson, the British entrepreneur and businessman, a tycoon who maintains a respectable position in Britain's rich lists, is a great example of someone who has reached high and far and still doesn't stop dreaming for a moment. Virgin, the brand he established, is broadening boundaries and changing its face all the time, and under its wide umbrella, there is already a record label, an airline, a train company, a communication conglomerate, a credit card company, a beverage brand name, a publishing house, and much more.

Branson has broken personal and professional records. He took record-breaking hot air balloon rides, sailed oceans, and galloped into the sunset on both sides of the globe. Now he is dreaming about traveling to space.

Although he takes his dreams extremely seriously, Branson makes sure to spice up his life with lightness and humor. For example, when he lost a bet, he honored his promise to work as a flight attendant for the competing airline. He shaved his legs, put on a female uniform, boarded the plane as a flight attendant, and served beverages to the surprised passengers. He doesn't hesitate to try new things and to be accessible. He uses his fortune to realize dreams one after the other and doesn't forget to donate to others as well. It seems like he is not afraid of changing his dreams while he moves. I have a feeling he is well in touch with the dreaming child he once was.

53 | KEEP YOUR FLEXIBILITY

We are dynamic creatures. Our dreams change in the course of our lives, just as our opinions do.

Not long ago, I revisited the original list I published in the blog. There were items that I had I changed over time.

I had given up on getting my high school diploma, which had seemed relevant to me at the time. It doesn't anymore. After all, I've managed just fine so far, so it seems reasonable that I'll keep doing just fine without it. I replaced this item with another: "To have my book translated into English and published abroad." The book you are now holding is the materialization of that dream. By the way, the translator found me and offered her services through Facebook.

Studying the French language? That's very nice. It's definitely a romantic and challenging language, but as a resident of the Middle East and as an activist in an organization that promotes Jewish-Arab coexistence, I decided that studying Arabic is much more important. Today, I already babble a few sentences in broken Arabic and do not listen to the skeptics around me.

Some of my tasks I have managed to perform, and some I haven't. The end of the world is not here yet. By the way, following the international lecturing invitations, I recently started to practice English, to improve my language skills. This is an example of how reality can interfere with and improve our list of dreams.

☑

I bumped into an acquaintance of mine on the street who apparently was following my blog.

"So, what about Oprah?" he asked sarcastically. "Have you guys met for coffee yet?"

"Not yet," I answered. "It will happen when it happens."

People are rightfully afraid to publish their dreams, exactly because of this kind of sarcastic remark that they may hear in the street, or during a family dinner. "So what's going on with that list of yours?"

I answer that a list is a living thing, which updates from time to time according to the wishes of the heart and the changing reality. Our dreams need to be realistic for us, remember?

So, yes, I have learned to forgive myself, out of the understanding that some things will be much easier to accomplish at different times. I also learned to forgive the cynics and the skeptics out of the understanding that this is a part of the cost of exposure and self-fulfillment.

It took me two years to launch my business website. One day it just happened. But what exactly happened to get me to that day? I met the right person for the job.

Some may say that "the universe" sent him to me. I choose to believe that I was attentive enough at the right moment to recognize that he was the professional I was waiting for. There is not one doubt in my mind that one day I will go back to my dream of speaking French, and when I do, it will be easier for me to learn it. When the student is ready, the teacher will appear.

While it is true that the list is a contract I signed with myself, at the same time, it is a sort of outline for action and as such, it is flexible. I call it "self-leniency." Others call it "going with the flow."

You are also cordially invited to flow with your own list.

Have you found along the way that one of the items is not doing it for you anymore? That it doesn't make you want to go the whole nine yards with it? No problem, no harm done. Update your list again and again. It's a breathing thing.

54 | HOW CAN A CONTRACT
BE FLEXIBILE?

The list is, indeed, a contract. However, it is a very personal one, as opposed to a union contract or a standard form contract. In my contract there are many loopholes that enable me to change the items of my list from time to time.

THE LIST IS MY LIFE'S GAME. IT'S MY SPECIAL MONOPOLY AND CHECKERS, WITH MY OWN RULES THAT I'VE COME UP WITH ON MY OWN, IN ORDER TO LEAD ME TO A PERSONAL VICTORY.

One evening not long ago, Shira pulled a card game named Coucou Taki down from her shelf and asked me to play with her. I didn't know the game, and although it is based on a very popular Israeli card game, it has some additional rules to follow. Shira explained them to me. You have to imitate the sound of the animal on the card that you put down, you can't make a sound when the animal on the card is colored red, and when you put down a lion card you have to say: "Hello, your majesty." However, while playing, her rules became very liquid. They kept changing conveniently when it helped her win.

Some would say that little Shira was trying to cheat, but I observed her behavior with a big smile on my face. My daughter wanted to beat me in the game, and in order for that to happen, she demonstrated an impressive flexibility in either inventing her own rules or circumventing an existing one.

I do not see it as deception, manipulation, or an alarming lack of integrity, but as a natural, childish behavior that has not yet been suppressed or amended into the "right" behavior forced on them by adults.

I do not think that Shira or Noga, my daughters, are any different from other sweet children I know. Our children are our true teachers; their behavior is authentic, direct, and emotional, with no defenses and redundant codes like we grownups develop.

TAKE SOME TIME TO LOOK AT THE LITTLE CHILDREN AROUND YOU—YOUR OWN CHILDREN, YOUR GRANDCHILDREN OR LITTLE RELATIVES AND TRY TO FIGURE OUT WHAT YOU HAVE LOST ON YOUR JOURNEY TO ADULTHOOD. IF YOU ARE STUCK FOR ANSWERS, ASK THE CHILD YOU ONCE WERE WHAT THEY THINK ABOUT YOUR CURRENT SITUATION, AND WHAT THEY WOULD HAVE DONE IN YOUR PLACE. KEEP THE CHILD THAT IS NESTLED WITHIN YOUR ADULT SOUL. HE WILL CONNECT YOU TO YOUR MOST SECRET DREAMS.

Just like that sign that says "Every number is a winner!" at the fairground or the amusement park, I feel that each one of my lists is a winner. Even if I changed a few items along the way, or didn't go all the way to achieving one of my items, I have still won. I have learned what doesn't really interest me, what doesn't move me all the way, and what doesn't work my motivational muscles. The knowledge of what I don't want, what I no longer wish for, is just as important as the understanding of what I do want to do.

There is a song by the Israeli singer/songwriter **Dudu Tasa** (co-written with **Tali Katz**) that says: "A grand failure is much better than dreams in the drawer." This is exactly how I feel. I prefer the feeling of failure to the feeling of missing something because I have never tried for it.

There are many examples out there of inventions that came to creation due to a mistake, as a part of a workplace accident, or a local failure that led to a breakthrough. Penicillin, for example, was discovered by a stroke of fate. Alexander Fleming performed research on the properties of staphylococci and used Petri dishes for his cultures. One day, he found that the germs on one of his dishes died and wondered how it happened. He found that one of his assistants had washed the dishes and left a water spot on one of them, which grew a fungus that killed the germs. This is how antibiotics, which changed the face of modern medicine, were invented.

Another such accidental success story is the one of Post-Its. In the early 1970s, Dr. Spencer Silver tried to develop bigger, stronger, tougher adhesives (according to the company's website). He failed, but inadvertently invented reusable sticky notes. At the end of the 1970s, the Post-Its hit the market and within a decade, they had become one of the most purchased office supplies in the world.

TRIAL AND ERROR, TRIAL AND WONDER, TRIAL AND PONDER: JUST AS THESE TWO INVENTORS AND MANY OTHERS HAVE PROVEN, A FAILED EXPERIMENT MAY LEAD TO AN EVEN BIGGER DISCOVERY.

I learned the importance of trying simply for the sake of gaining experience at a young age, thanks to my mother. When moving up from elementary school to high school, I was asked to choose my focus subject. Considering the acting talent I had demonstrated since a young age, it was clear to me that I was going to study acting. Minutes away from my home, in the town of Bat Yam, there was a school that offered a well-established and successful theatre program that produced many actors who later integrated into show business. However, I had my eyes set on the leading drama school in another town called Thelma Yellin. For months, I practiced for my audition with help of one of the most esteemed acting teachers in Israel at the time.

A day before the exams, I went to an open house held by my neighborhood school and decided that this was where I wanted to go to school. I felt it was right for me to stay within the circle of my friends from elementary school, and that I'd rather pass on the daily commute, and that I didn't really need to attend that much anticipated audition after all.

My mother was the one who eventually convinced me otherwise, saying: "Don't pass on the audition. On the contrary, do it, and if you pass, you'll have the power to choose your path. You'll also spare yourself the feeling of a missed opportunity that might stay with you for the rest of your life."

I listened to my wise mother, took the audition for Thelma Yellin, and decided to forfeit my placement and attend the local high school.

This was when I adopted this approach, and it has become my norm.

DON'T SAY, "I HAVE FAILED" OR "I HAVE SUCCEEDED." ONLY SAY, "I HAVE PLAYED."

This insight has led me to another rule that is helping me realize my lists.

55 | DON'T SAY NO, ## SAY YES

In the course of my journey I have received thousands of emails from readers who wanted to share their stories and lists with me, bring certain notes to my attention, enlighten me, give advice, offer cooperation, help, or just drink coffee together. Some of them had brilliant ideas for promoting some of my list items, questions, or objections. Others wanted to interest me in a partnership in their future business, ask for my help in phrasing their list, or just sent indecent proposals.

I have met them all. I always say "Yes" and meet for a quick coffee. Best case scenario—it will lead to amazing results. Worst case—I will have wasted an hour of my life.

You too will find that on your way to realizing your list, you will correspond with many people, knock on many different doors, and try to initiate meetings that will help you progress. People may contact you as well. My advice to you is to always agree to such meetings. During my personal and professional life, I have gained some rare partnerships and friendships, thanks to conversations that began on social networks.

SAYING "NO" TO THE ABUNDANCE OF OPPORTUNITIES AND INFORMATION AT OUR DISPOSAL IS A KIND OF SIN AGAINST OURSELVES. WE COMMIT THE SIN OF TAKING A NEGATIVE ATTITUDE ON A DAILY BASIS, WITHOUT EVEN BEING AWARE OF IT.

When I sit with my single friend who I have previously mentioned, and we surf the dating website where she signed on to, I notice the negative approach that characterizes the messages in these website. Hundreds of people who are looking for love and trying to connect with each other write a lot of restrictive demands and just plainly negative messages. We came across so many descriptions and demands such as non-smoker, not overweight, no divorcees, no chatterboxes. Messages such as "Please! I'm exhausted from being here, giving it a last chance" and so on.

Why be negative? The word "no" has no attraction or sex appeal to it and neither do those who frequently use it.

56 | ALLOW YOURSELF TO
BE SELFISH (IN MODERATION)

One of the most moving lectures I had the pleasure of giving took place in the culturally mixed city of Haifa, where Arabs and Jews co-reside. The lecture took place in a place called Beit HaGefen (The Vine House), where cultural activities are regularly held, connecting Jews and Arabs.

I was invited to speak on a day that was dedicated to women and the auditorium was full of hundreds of participants, mostly elderly Arab women. Some of them had never sat in front of a computer, let alone used Facebook or blogged. Many of them didn't understand Hebrew very well, and had to ask their friends to translate what I was saying.

Although The List started as an Internet experiment, they quickly connected to the idea and to the notion of speaking out their dreams. Many of them asked to share their charming, very modest dreams with the rest of the women.

One of the things that kept coming up during the conversation was the fact that most of them had sacrificed their chance of self-fulfillment on the altar of raising their children and caring for their homes and husbands, as part of their society's conservative tradition.

When one of the women spoke of her dream of touring the United States with her close friend, I urged her to open a savings account and to mark a goal for herself—to fly to New York within two years. She looked down and said it wasn't realistic since she had children to care for. When I asked how old the kids were, she replied: "Twenty-three and twenty-five." Her motherly commitment impressed and upset me at the same time.

A FULFILLED PARENT IS A MUCH HAPPIER PARENT, AND A HAPPIER PARENT IS A BETTER-FUNCTIONING PARENT.

When I was in my twenties one of my closest friends was about to get married and become a mother. Out of genuine parental dedication and sheer excitement, she decided to drop out of her MA studies and leave the prestigious and lucrative job she had landed when she got her first degree.

"I decided to be a stay-home mother for at least two years. I want to give my daughter all the tender, loving care she needs," she said to me. We used to meet every other week for a morning coffee and conversations about breast-feeding, nappy-changing and her life as a new mother. Gradually I started noticing how her energy and joy were slowly replaced by fatigue, sadness, and finally frustration and anger. In one of our conversations, after about a year-and-a-half, she confided in me that she was having a serious crisis with her husband and thoughts of divorcing him were already creeping in. She was totally lost, and had no clear idea how her dream of a happy family had so quickly shattered to pieces.

A few hours after that sad conversation I called her and said, "I know why everything is falling apart! You have completely wiped yourself out of the equation! You have lost yourself somewhere between the cooking pots, nappy changing, and your pygmies. Tomorrow morning you're going to wake up, get dressed, put a bit of make-up on and start looking for a job. Any job. You have to start meeting people your age again, experience things, dream dreams and bring them back home."

She followed my advice and things at home started to pick up again. Her relationship with her husband was back on the right track.

My friend's experience was very significant for me too, since it made me understand how important it is to be a fulfilled parent. Only a happy parent can raise happy children.

☑️

I found another example of this in the safety video they show right before the plane takes off: "During the flight if the cabin pressure changes, an oxygen mask will drop automatically from the panel above you. Remain seated, pull the mask toward you, and use the support strap to hold the mask over your mouth and nose. If you are traveling with a child, put on your own mask before assisting another person," the narrator says in a calming voice.

Before becoming a parent, I didn't understand the reason behind this instruction. Doesn't the child's safety take precedence over ours? Isn't it more appropriate to take care of the child first? And then it hit me—it's the other way around! Only when I'm calm and relaxed can I dedicate myself to taking care of my children.

I have adopted this safety instruction and have been practicing it in my daily life.

As a part of my work as an interviewer I fly overseas several times a year. Since Shira and Noga were born, those work trips are accompanied by parental guilt trips, to the extent that I sometimes considered giving up on an interview and staying home, close to them. That was until I understood that those trips are my overseas "oxygen supply." Together with the presents I bring back and especially the stories about all those faraway places—worth just as much as a father who reads bedtime stories every night. I'm a fulfilled parent (although sometimes an absent one), and therefore, I hope, a better parent.

Some words in our language receive unjustified negative publicity. A few examples are "manipulation," "boundaries," "interest," and "egoism."

A friend of mine once complained to me that her husband didn't take any part in the household chores and that she was tired of cleaning, cooking, washing, folding laundry, and taking care of the children and the pets.

"Set some boundaries then," I suggested to her.

She looked at me with dismay. "He's not my child! He's my husband. Why would I set him boundaries?"

"Because some things are too much and you're not willing to take them anymore," I explained. "'Boundaries' is not a word reserved for children. It applies to adults too."

For some reason, the word "boundaries" is perceived as a negative thing when said in regard to adults. The word "ego," too. It's true that an untamed, self-centered ego is usually attributed to people you don't want to spend time with, but I don't see anything wrong with thinking about ourselves first every once in a while. Sometimes, in order to stay true to ourselves, we need to stop thinking about other people for a little bit.

Just as our parents instilled false beliefs in us (we shouldn't ask for help, we shouldn't share our secret wishes such as birthday ones or wishes we make upon seeing a shooting star), we embraced the terrible notion that we are not allowed to think of ourselves first.

IF WE DON'T THINK OF OURSELVES, WHO IS GOING TO DO IT FOR US?

I invite you to think of yourselves and your dreams (provided they don't hurt anybody else, of course) so that you become better parents, better spouses, better sons and daughters to your parents, and better friends. As I said, children learn by imitating their parents more than they learn by being told what to do, so a martyred parent who gives up his desires, needs, and dreams is actually raising his children to be unfulfilled people.

While it is true that dedicating yourself to your family may delay some of your dreams to an extent, it is also true that your family can accompany you on your journey to realizing your dreams and help you in your journey.

My desired trip to Australia has been postponed due to family matters. However, I have no doubt in my mind that I will realize it within the next few years. I may take the whole family on a road, or I may go alone for a shorter period. Either way I will not feel guilty, since technology enables us to stay in touch on a daily basis even when we are far away.

We no longer live in times when the holiday postcards we send from abroad reach home two months after we have already returned and unpacked. Today, you can be on the other side of the world and communicate via Skype, Viber, WhatsApp, and of course via news websites, television, and Facebook.

IN ORDER TO REALIZE YOUR LIST, I INVITE YOU TO FIRST THINK ABOUT YOUR DESIRES AND DREAMS. REALIZING THEM WILL MAKE YOU HAPPIER, MORE FULFILLED AND ROUNDED PEOPLE.

I BELIEVE THAT EVERYTHING IS SURMOUNTABLE. ALMOST EVERYTHING. EVERY TECHNICAL, ECONOMIC, OR CONSCIENCE-RELATED PROBLEM IS SOLVABLE THROUGH ASKING FOR HELP FROM RELEVANT PEOPLE OR PLACES.

---

57 | THE POWER OF A
WRITTEN MIRROR

A list is not only a road map, an outline, and a personal contract. It is also a mirror that reflects your inner self to yourself and to the world.

A list has just as much power as a psychologist who sits in front of a patient reflecting the ways in which he handles his life back at him. If you are attentive and aware of the words you wrote on the paper, first as a draft and then after processing, you will be able to learn quite a bit about yourself. This is why I'm a big believer in a written list of dreams that is hanging in front of our face instead of rolling somewhere in our head, or on a digital memo in our mobile phone, alongside thousands of notes and pictures.

In the digital reality we live in, when computers and mobile phones have become for many of us bare essentials, writing a list with a pen on a paper is a kind of a ceremonial effort that is all about doing something for yourself. It's not just the time you dedicate to it, but the attention you finally give to what is going on in your head. An external look at the written items will enable you to work your senses and observe your dreams from a fresh point of view.

More than once I've heard very touching items like, "Tell my parents I love them more often," "Visit Grandma in the nursing home," and similar wishes that came out of their heads or hearts without thinking about them first.

An effective list can even change our behavior. Many believe that they are too old to change, but it's never too late to add one negative trait or pattern to your list that you would be glad to eliminate or even just weaken, and start working toward that.

I can testify that my lists helped me control my anger levels and led me to a behavioral change.

When I was twenty-five, after a stressful and dynamic period participating in the setting up of a new newspaper, I traveled to London for a holiday. I left angry and disappointed because one of my editors gave a story, which I had started working on, to another reporter. Sitting in Green Park in London and updating my list, I added the item, "Not get mad so often."

I went back to Israel and noticed that for about a week I actually got angry a lot less than before. After about a week I went back to my normal, angry self again.

Fatefully, two months later I traveled again from work. This time it was Greece. Once again, I compiled a list and once again I wrote "Not get mad so often." This time it lasted for a whole month.

That year, I wrote five different lists of goals and updated them frequently. In general, it was a year of professional and personal breakthrough for me.

While writing my fifth list for that year, I found myself writing that very familiar item: "Not get mad so often."

I looked at that white paper that reflected my heart's wishes and became upset with myself.

"Don't you see that it bothers you? That your anger is holding you back?" I scolded myself. "Don't get mad so much!"

These inner dialogues and the fact that I recognized a pattern which was written in front of my eyes time and again, in black and white, caused me to stop getting so mad by the end of that year.

This doesn't mean that I have become a Buddhist monk who is immune to annoying situations—just put me on the phone with my Internet provider and I'll get mad in seconds! It just means that my anger no longer takes charge of me.

I can be extremely angry about something, but I get over it quickly and it doesn't follow me around like a shadow. I no longer wallow in my anger for days over negligible issues and nonsense and it is so much better!

Many list writers have shared with me the ways in which their list has helped them change their behavior. One young man, for example, told me how he became more communicative in his relationships. Another man told me how his list helped him comply with his wife's request that he show more affection and romance in their relationship. A woman told me how she stopped thinking of others first and started to put herself at the top of her list. As a result, she is flying next summer to participate in the annual Burning Man Festival in Nevada.

THE LIST HAS THE POWER TO CHANGE OUR BEHAVIOR AND TURN US INTO BETTER PEOPLE. DEDICATE AT LEAST ONE ITEM IN YOUR FINAL LIST TO MAKING SUCH CHANGES.

---

58 | LIFE'S SPEED BUMPS

Even with all the optimism and positive energy I advocate, there is no doubt that life is complicated and sometimes hits us with unpleasant surprises. These often draw energy from us that in other circumstances we could have used to advance ourselves.

An engine malfunction in the car causes an unexpected expense that will cost us our annual vacation. A loved one is sick and while caring for her, we neglect other important chores. Pay cuts or layoffs require tightening the belt and even the political situation can sometimes have implications on us.

IN ORDER NOT TO DROWN WHEN THE GOING GETS TOUGH, WE MUST TRY TO KEEP OUR ENERGY RESOURCES AND OUR MOTIVATION HIGH EVEN IN PERIODS WHEN WE ARE NOT AS PERKY AS USUAL.

During my military service I was a commander in the Air Force's Commanders School. Over the course of my service I handled many cases of soldiers who were unmotivated and didn't want to be serving in that base. There were desertion attempts, depressions, hysteria, and even one suicide attempt.

One of the tools my fellow commanders gave me was what called the "Is Everything Really That Bad?!" conversation.

I would sit in front of a depressed, disgruntled soldier and try to persuade him that there are two sides to every coin. It would go like this:

Soldier: "I want to leave this base. I'm miserable here!"

Me: "Wait! Is everything bad here? Isn't there even one good thing you can say about this base?"

Soldier: "Well, the other soldiers are pretty cool, but the base's location is terrible!"

Me: "OK. Got it. So socially everything is good. About the location, isn't it nice that it is so close to Eilat?" (Eilat is a coastal tourist town and Israel's southernmost point. It is often referred to as the "Las Vegas of Israel.")

Soldier: "Yes, sure, it's cool, but the weekly commute here is killing me! I live in the center of Israel and every weekend I have to travel for six hours just to visit my parents."

Me: "Not every weekend. Every second weekend. And besides, what about the swimming pool in the compound? Don't you enjoy it?"

Soldier: "Yes of course I enjoy it. I actually told my brother about the pool and he couldn't believe me! His army base certainly doesn't have one."

Me: "Right. Don't forget about the mini mall too. So let's see—you're content with your friends, you go to Eilat often, and you have a swimming pool. So where's the bad part?"

This is where the first crack in the negativity wall would usually appear and things might take a positive turn.

I didn't fool myself into believing that this short conversation might solve everyone's problems, but I'm sure that it infused at least a bit of warmth and positive energy in him.

TRY HAVING THE "IS EVERYTHING BAD?" CONVERSATION WITH YOURSELF FROM TIME TO TIME.

59 | THE LITTLE
NOTEPAD

Along my journey to self-fulfillment I encountered many speed bumps. One of my businesses suffered a grave economic blow, my dear grandmother passed away and my third novel consisted of only seven chapters for months. Still, even in the worst moments I managed to find energy and strength thanks to my family and close friends and supporters, as well as a little notepad that I've had on my bed since I was sixteen. That notepad enables me to ask myself every day: Is Everything Bad? And reply immediately, even on the harder days: Actually, it's all pretty good!

It's just a little notepad that rapidly fills up, in which I write every night five things that made my day.

Don't worry, it's not a new list. It's a different tool, something to help you along.

What kind of things make my day? It can be a great dessert I ate, a new café I've discovered, an inspiring book I've read, an autumn breeze that cooled me down, a heart-to-heart conversation with a friend, a good laughter I shared with my daughter and, of course, a refreshing afternoon nap.

I sometimes enjoy retrieving one of my old notepads and reading about the things that made me happy five years earlier. It seems that with time, my brain has been indoctrinated. It can recognize in seconds when something good is happening. After all, these great moments are all we have. Every time we don't recognize a moment, it swiftly turns into nothing but a memory.

STRIKE WHILE THE IRON IS HOT, REMEMBER?

Today I can find five good things even on my worst days. This is how well I have learned to locate those little oxygen tanks that are dispersed around us, and use them.

While doing that, or maybe as a result of that, I find the mental strength to keep going ahead at full capacity toward executing my lists.

I practice positive thinking with my daughter Shira at bedtime too. I ask her to choose the two good things that happened to her that day.

"You let me eat ice cream even though it was raining and we watched *Frozen* twice."

Naturally, as a young child her experiences may be limited, but she is gradually learning to appreciate things. She is a smart child, and she is internalizing my life's philosophy. She already knows that she should speak her wishes out loud, in front of her parents, because it increases the chances that they will come true.

Now she knows how to write and, following my suggestion to write her own list of dreams, she wrote a list in her childish handwriting and hung it on her bedroom door.

☐ Go to Jerusalem

☐ Prepare ice cream based on my great-grandmother's recipe

☐ Get a Disney princess costume

☐ Learn to speak English

☐ Spend more time with friends

On second thought, maybe I should have waited with my suggestion until Shira is in her twenties, since now my checking account is under a real existential threat.

60 | A THANK YOU
LIST

If you are honest, you will agree with what I'm about to say. If you are not as honest, you may resist it at first, but then you too will nod your head in agreement.

WE ENJOY WHINING! IN FACT, IT'S ONE OF OUR FAVORITE PRACTICES.

We complain, sometimes without a real reason, about our spouses, children, work, and life in general.

I hope you will embrace the little notepad idea, and that you will always find good things to write in it before going to bed. I hope that your little notepad will help you complain less and perpetuate the energy from the positive little moments that come our way daily.

I believe that it is important to get used to cherishing and appreciating our achievements, big and small alike, every day, all the time.

Each one of us has a list of achievements that we can take credit for. Each of us should thank ourself for moments of courage that brought on a change in our life. One woman overcame the fear of what people would say and had breast implants, which made her very happy. A man decided to invest his money in the stock market and loved the adrenaline rush of the profession, so he decided to change his profession. A lawyer decided to leave her job and pursue a career in design. A family decided to drop out of the rat race and go on a one-year family trip around the world.

You too should get used to practicing gratitude for what you have achieved and for some of the blessed characteristics that made you what you are and helped you achieve so much. Stop thinking about more dreams that are awaiting you for just one second and dedicate a few more minutes to yet another list. Have you noticed I like lists?

HI THERE. GET READY TO MEET YOUR GRATITUDE LIST.

Write the substantial things you have achieved in your life (they don't have to be grand) and for which you are grateful. Mention the things you have materialized, that have given you pleasure and joy and you will never forget. (If you do you can always go back to the list and be reminded of them.)

When the list is full take a look at it.

I hope you feel deeply proud of yourself, and that your eyes well up with tears of satisfaction.

1.

2.

3.

4.

5.

6.

7.

8.

9.

10.

"SHOWING GRATITUDE IS ONE OF THE SIMPLEST, YET MOST POWERFUL, THINGS HUMANS CAN DO FOR EACH OTHER."

(RANDY PAUSCH)

11.

12.

13.

14.

15.

16.

17.

18.

19.

20.

"GRATITUDE IS A MEMORY OF THE HEART."

(JEAN MASSIEU)

21.

22.

23.

24.

25.

26.

27.

28.

29.

30.

You got all the way to the end? That's impressive! These are all the things you have achieved so far.

There is no reason why you can't realize your new list of dreams. I'm talking about the focused and effective list that you will compile by the end of this book. True, it's not always going to be easy, there are going to be bumps along the way, but hey, this is your way. If you've managed to do so many amazing things so far, then . . .

WHAT IS THE PROBLEM
WITH WRITING
ONE
MORE LIST OF DREAMS?

61 | THE SECOND LIST THAT SAVED ME

The first list, the one that saved me, I composed during a period in which I was paralyzed and in a wheelchair.

I have written many lists since then. Many of them have saved me, helped me progress, and turned me into a much more pleasant man to myself and to everyone around me.

It was at the age of thirty-four that I got yet another reminder of the power of the list, sharing it, and publishing it.

It happened when I was in Oslo, as part of an activity that brings together Israeli and Palestinian artists in order to create a common cultural agenda. It was in the middle of singing hymns of peace that my phone started ringing. They were all calls from Israel. On the line were suppliers who provided goods to my stores. They all had complaints.

✔ **You haven't paid me in two months!**

✔ **Where's my check?**

✔ **Why haven't you paid us rent in the last six months?**

Upon receiving the tenth call, I understood there was a serious problem. I contacted my people back home and found out that an enormous amount of money, almost a quarter of a million shekels, had disappeared from my business account.

I immediately returned home to take charge of my sinking ship, and quickly realized how deeply in trouble I was. Someone who was involved in the business took advantage of my absence, of my involvement in other projects, and my lack of experience in business management and withdrew money, changed registrations, stole merchandise, made false promises to suppliers and clients, and caused huge damages to the business. Damages that eventually I had to mend.

Even dozens of little lists won't cheer up a person in such a dire situation. All of my positive thinking had turned into empty slogans. I had no idea how to restore my self-confidence and generate positive energy.

I felt frightened and completely lost. I feared that all of my personal and professional achievements were going to be wiped out now with dozens of creditors waving their claims for their lost monies at me.

I imagined leaving my beautiful apartment. I imagined the tarnishing of my good reputation that I had worked so hard to establish once the scandal leaked to the gossip columns.

I started making my peace with having to give up vacations, dining out, and shopping sprees for the next few years.

Eventually I decided to take action. I put aside the original list I posted on the blog and wrote an emergency list:

- ☐ Email them a summary of our conversation
- ☐ Call all my suppliers and personally explain the situation to them
- ☐ Consult with a lawyer
- ☐ Check an option for a loan to cover for the missing sum
- ☐ Talk to friends who own a business
- ☐ Ask close friends for a loan
- ☐ Speak with people who got into debt and managed to overcome it

These were some of the items in that emergency list. The next step was to make the list public in spite of the difficulty in exposing and admitting a failure.

You know me by now and you know I'm a big believer in publicity and asking for help in every situation from both close and distant people.
I posted a short, vague status on my Facebook page.

Yuval Abramovitz
about an hour ago

"One of my businesses got into a financial entanglement. A large amount of money has disappeared and I'm looking for solutions. If you have creative ideas or have experienced something of the same nature, if you are a lawyer or know a lawyer and if you have something that will make me smile right now—you're welcome to share it with me."

In a matter of five minutes, there were already hundreds of comments to the post and more than 200 private messages. Here are some of them:

✔ **You lost a quarter of a million shekels? That's peanuts. I had a business that accumulated a debt of millions and I solved the crisis within two years.**

✔ **Talk to your bank and ask to spread out your original loan over a longer period of time and to get another loan to fill the hole.**

✔ **If your company is limited, you can "lift the veil." Your creditors will see that there is no money there to reclaim.**

✔ **You are not liable for the debts of the company. Your creditors cannot sue you personally.**

✔ **Sue the person who stole the money.**

✔ **Close the business and open a new one that will cover for the losses.**

✔ **I'm a lawyer and would gladly represent you for half the usual price.**

There were hundreds of responses and all of them, without exception, led me to believe I could solve this unlucky situation.

I kept reporting my situation in public until one day, I found myself having a conversation with a switched-on lawyer who asked me if I believed in the power and economic potential of my business. When I said I did, he suggested that we fight for the future of my business in court, remove the sabotaging person, and recover the lost money.

I agreed and we entered a legal process that took four months. These were long and nerve-racking months, during which the tables turned over and over, until eventually, I won.

The sabotaging person had been removed from the business, which was now solely mine; most of the money was returned in numerous payments (as of now there are two more years of payments remaining); I achieved a settlement with my creditors and earned their trust again.

After another six months of financial and emotional rehabilitation, I started working to establish another business, and after six more months, another one. I do not wish that kind of an experience upon anyone, but in retrospect it led me to personal, emotional, and financial growth. Today, I'm a much more resilient businessman (at least mentally). A phone call from the bank telling me I have exceeded my credit by 2000 shekels doesn't make me lose sleep. What's ILS2,000 after you've lost a quarter of a million? Peanuts.

There were many reasons why I succeeded in getting out of that horrible turbulence. One of the main ones was the list that helped me focus, the clear steps I defined for myself, publishing my list, and my mental ability to ask for help.

More than once, we encounter obstacles and circumstances that hold us back in the process of self-fulfillment. We must remember that our way of dealing with the unexpected stems from the quality of the list we compile. The more efficient our list is, the better we will overcome the obstacles in our way.

☑

An Israeli who resides in Canada and was exposed to my blog through my Facebook page asked to share a modest dream of hers which was put on hold because of a car accident. Here is her letter:

I had a dream: to take a scuba diving course. Back in 2003, after having played with the idea for a while, I decided to finally take the step and do it.

I asked friends, got recommendations and chose the club where I was going to take the course. I called them and spoke to an agent about the details, the conclusion of the conversation being that once I'd booked a hotel room for the duration of the course, I would call her back to pay in order to secure my space.

That was on a Thursday. On the weekend, I put it off till I got to work. I'd do it then.

I had all the time in the world, didn't I?

On our way to work, my husband and I were involved in a car accident. I was hit with the seat belt, right in the clavicle, which made breathing or laughing a hard task to perform. Even just sitting up was extremely painful. At night, whenever I turned around in my sleep, the pain woke me up. Considering the condition I was in, scuba diving was completely out of the question.

Like anything in life, the accident also had a positive side to it. When I was examined in the hospital they found out the reason I wasn't getting pregnant although we had been married and trying for three and a half years. A month after the accident, I was already pregnant for the first time. Naturally, scuba diving was cast aside once again.

Four months after I had my first girl, I was pregnant with the second one. When she was born, I had just started studying for my master's degree and then I started a new job, and then another pregnancy and another job and when my third one was a year old, we moved to Canada and were already expecting our fourth.

A decade passed and the scuba diving dream kept moving further and further down my busy list of priorities.

In February 2013 I started following you on Facebook. With time the spirit of your blog caught on to me and I really connected with the message that you need to shout out your dreams and live in the moment. Those insights started to seep in and during my visit to Israel last summer, I started to think about my dream again.

First came the negativity and polite upbringing: it's not fair to leave my mom with four kids for a week just to go to Eilat with an air tank on my back. It's going to be hard for her, there are four of them, after all! But how could I ask my husband to spend his vacation babysitting, when he only has ten days. And they kept on coming.

I DIDN'T STAY SILENT THIS TIME. I SHOUTED OUT MY DREAM.

Well, not exactly shouted. I mumbled it in my husband's ear. His response was "No problem. When I get there you can go take the course."

My mother also said she would help. I decided to take an Open Water course which is shorter and instead of doing it in the Red Sea in Eilat, I did it in the Mediterranean, so I could come back home every day. Finally, after ten years of thinking about it, my dream came true.

For my next visit, I shouted out my dream and this time, my cousin agreed to come to Eilat with me for the weekend, to entertain my daughters while I went scuba diving, and so, here I am, going to make the second part of my dream come true and get an advanced adventurer certificate. Baby steps and shouting my dreams made it come true. The next part of my dream is to go dive in an exotic destination: Hawaii, the Caribbean or the Maldives.

Today I know it will happen. Nothing can keep me from realizing my dreams.

62 | BIGGER THAN LIFE
LISTS

If you go back to your first, unprocessed list, you will find that many of the items that you wrote can be defined as "super objectives." Just to remind you, those are not items that outline the steps you have to take in order to achieve your super objectives, but rather big dreams, that take big chunks of life to realize and cannot be realized in a year or two.

In the coming pages you will find blank space to document "theme lists" according to categories and subjects. As opposed to the immediate goals you will want to execute in the next two years, these are places to write what I call "super lists" with all the items that you will want to achieve during your lifetime, without setting a deadline or an estimated date.

The purpose of these lists is to broaden your thinking and enrich your bag of dreams.

You are welcome to fill the next pages, copy items from them into your final list for the next year, update your items from time to time, and get ideas for your future annual lists.

THE BOOKS I WANT TO READ

THE MOVIES I HAVE NOT WATCHED YET AND MUST WATCH

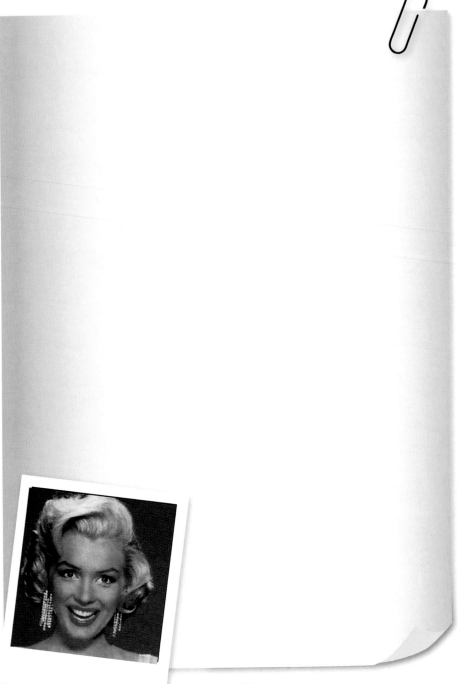

THE CITIES AND COUNTRIES I WANT TO TRAVEL TO

RESTAURANTS AROUND THE WORLD
WHERE I WANT TO EAT

THE CRAZY THINGS I WANT TO DO

THE MUSEUMS I WANT TO VISIT

PLACES AROUND THE WORLD THAT I WANT TO SEE

THE MUSIC ALBUMS I MISSED BUT I MUST LISTEN TO

COURSES I WANT TO TAKE

FEARS I WANT TO OVERCOME

TELEVISION SERIES I WANT TO CATCH UP ON

THINGS I WOULD LIKE TO DO FOR MY HOUSE

THE ORGANIZATIONS AND CAUSES I WANT TO VOLUNTEER FOR

PEOPLE WITH WHOM I WOULD LOVE TO HAVE A HEART-TO-HEART CONVERSATION

PEOPLE I WOULD LOVE TO RECONNECT WITH

PERFORMANCES I WOULD LIKE TO SEE

EXTREME CHALLENGES I WOULD LIKE TO TRY

THE TASKS I WOULD BE RELIEVED TO COMPLETE

FAMILY MEMBERS, FRIENDS AND ACQUAINTANCES TO WHOM I WOULD LIKE TO EXPRESS MY LOVE

THE GIFTS I WANT TO BUY MYSELF

THE GIFTS I WANT TO BUY OTHERS

TRAITS I WOULD LIKE TO IMPROVE IN MYSELF

TRAITS I WOULD LOVE TO GET RID OF

HABITS I WOULD LOVE TO ADOPT

THINGS I WOULD LIKE TO DO FOR MY HEALTH

THINGS I WILL DO WHEN I HAVE MORE MONEY

INSPIRING PEOPLE I WOULD LIKE TO MEET

HOBBIES I WOULD LIKE TO TAKE UP

MISTAKES I WOULD NOT LIKE TO REPEAT

THINGS I WOULD LIKE TO DO ON MY NEXT BIRTHDAY

THINGS I WANT TO INVENT AND DEVELOP

INDULGENT PLACES AT WHICH I WOULD LIKE TO SPEND AT LEAST ONE NIGHT

WORLD EVENTS I WOULD LOVE TO ATTEND

THINGS I WOULD LIKE TO DO FOR MY FAMILY

SILLY THINGS I WOULD LIKE TO DO

TOXIC PEOPLE I WOULD LIKE TO CUT OUT OF MY LIFE

THINGS I WOULD LIKE TO DO ON MY NEXT DAYS OFF WORK

CRAFTS I WOULD LIKE TO TRY

SPORTS I WOULD LIKE TO GET BETTER AT

63 | YOUR FINAL LIST

Our mutual journey on the way to your effective list is about to end.

If you followed through all the stages as they appear in the book you now have quite a few lists and items.

Along with your 100 dreams list, you have forty shorter lists, according to specific subjects, from which you can draw ideas and items for the final list you will soon produce.

Go through your lists again, rewrite, accurately phrase and focus them.

Using the different lists you have written so far to guide you, copy items you want to achieve in the next few months. After that, you can write your final list for the next year.

Along with personal, family-related, and professional items, you should integrate social and global interests into your list in order to benefit from a well-balanced list and feel a sense of growth in all areas of your life.

In the next pages, you will find space for eleven more lists, which will comprise your final and refined list and will serve you in the upcoming years.

I suggest you write lists two to four times a year. When the pages fill up, buy a nice notebook and turn it into your designated The List book. You can go back to it every few months to refresh your lists, or purchase a new blank notebook and go through the experience all over again. You can do it on your birthday, on your favorite holiday, during your annual vacation, or at any given time during the year.

Date: / / / Hour:_____ Place:_____

Date: / / / Hour:_____ Place:_____

Date: / / /   Hour:_____ Place:_____

Date: / / /   Hour:_____ Place:_____

Date: / /   Hour:_____ Place:_____

Date: / / Hour:_____ Place:_____

Date: / / / Hour:_____ Place:_____

Date: / /   Hour:_____ Place:_____

64 A LISTING
PARTY

I wrote my old list, the one that led me to open *The List* blog, on New Year's Eve 2006, when I invited a group of close friends and asked them to write their lists and then share them with the others.

If you feel like you have connected with my philosophy, which encourages you to turn your list of dreams into public information, I invite you to organize annual list parties for friends, family, and colleagues (you can do them in your workplace too). Learn to know the people around you more intimately and see them in a different light. You are welcome, of course, to buy or pass them a copy of this book, so they can be as accurate as possible when writing their lists.

Teach your children to set annual goals for themselves. Guide them to write effective, realistic, focused, and modest lists. If they are too young to write, cut appropriate pictures from magazines and old newspapers or find them on the Internet and print them at home. Turn your immediate environment of family and friends into a listing and dream-expressing society.

In my lectures I sometimes meet people who have been working together for years and have mostly mundane, everyday conversations of blowing off steam about the boss, having political arguments, chatting about a television show, and so on. They hardly ever talk to each other about their dreams.

In my first lecture, given to the staff of the Open University, when the participants started reading their lists out loud, one person read out "Swim three times a week." Not a very complicated dream to realize, right?

Suddenly, another person jumped out of his seat and exclaimed: "I can't believe it! This is exactly what I've been wanting to do for years!"

The crowd roared with laughter. I didn't understand why everybody was laughing, until I learned that the two had been sharing a little office for the last ten years! If only they had shared their dreams with each other sooner, they could have been Olympic champions by now.

65 | WE ARE OUR OWN OBSTACLES

I have wanted to write this book for a long time. I wanted to summarize my *The List* journey and reflect on where it had taken me, to add cases I've witnessed during lectures, to tell about meetings and conversations with thousands of dreamers who wrote lists, and to distill the effective and operative steps I have taken, in order to pay them forward.

I wrote and wrote, page upon page, and they were all piled up in my computer. Again and again, I kept putting off taking the crucial step.

✔ **Why should people buy an inspirational book from me?**

✔ **What have I done in my life?**

✔ **What value do my thoughts have?**

✔ **No publisher will support me.**

✔ **I just hope people won't mistake it for preaching.**

✔ **I don't want to be considered a megalomaniac.**

An impressive array of negative thoughts and resistances flooded my mind. To my delight, I heard enough positive voices around me who supported me and helped me believe the value of the project.

One day, in a moment of partial unconsciousness and reduced inhibitions, I decided to publish the book independently. I fondly call it "a moment of complete stupidity" when I wasn't fully loaded with the usual obstructions and excuses, and I let myself be bold.

I've been following the wonders of crowdfunding websites for a while. Those websites follow the principal of "dream shouting." For the last few years, they have been growing around the world, enabling thousands of dreamers to share their ideas and inventions with the global village in order to raise the money to materialize them.

I asked myself if raising the money through the Internet is the right way to get funding for this book, which you are now reading. The answer rapidly came. Yes!

This book is the best proof of my theory—that the ideas that motivate *The List* actually work. In the next few pages, you will find tips and a toolbox that will help you raise money through the Internet in order to realize your dreams.

66 | BIG MONEY
COMES IN SMALL PORTIONS

This is the leading principal of crowdfunding: Big money comes in small portions.

First I'd like to explain how crowdfunding works. An artist or a group of artists starts a campaign page for their project and invites visitors to join the community that promotes its funding. The audience receives full value in return for their money, in the form of a product, a service, or an experience. For example: a preorder of the album or concert tickets, lectures, participating in a project, and so on.

After months of thorough research of the system I decided to open a campaign page to publish the book in Hebrew and in English. The campaign was launched on www.jumpstarter.co.il.

I shouted out my dream. I distributed the link to the campaign page using social media and emailed my friends. In the first twenty-four hours, I already had ILS36,000, more than 30 percent of my final goal. This amount doubled itself after forty-eight hours and on the third day, I already crossed the target budget and finished the day with 107 percent of it!

The fact that I managed to raise my entire target budget within three days opened me to an opportunity for which I wasn't prepared.

The excitement peaked when I suddenly realized that *The List* had a much bigger and more connected community than I ever estimated. I also suddenly had fifty-seven more days to raise more money. I was given a chance to play a game I hadn't planned. And I had to get ready for it on the spot!

67 | THE PROJECT AND I
EXTEND

After sixty days of ecstasy and severe sleep deprivation, the campaign ended. While the website clock was ticking the scoreboard showed the unimaginable amount raised: ILS251,818! Yes, more than a quarter of a million raised in just two months! That kind of money covered the publication of the book in Hebrew and in six other languages, and allowed us to invest in public relations and marketing—an important element in promoting a new product in our local Israeli cultural market, which suffers from a chronic lack of funds.

During the first two weeks of the campaign I was so excited I couldn't sleep. I felt like I was floating. Currents ran through my body and not metaphorically. I got an actual huge "like" from thousands of strangers. Some of them invested over $2,000 in my book! I envisaged myself as the frenzied broker Leonardo DiCaprio played in *The Wolf of Wall Street*. Every time I left the computer for a few minutes to eat lunch or shower, I'd come back and find out more supporters had joined and a thousand more shekels were invested into my campaign. Sometimes even tens of thousands.

The fear of failure and humiliation gave way to great happiness, accompanied by a rising sense of self and professional confidence and feeling that I had finally cemented my worldview.

My personal sense of victory was derived from conquering my fears. I did listen to my fears prior to the campaign, and they were more toxic than any other poison. But eventually I was able to break through the barrier and so can you.

How did I do it? Through meeting and conversing with people who understand crowdfunding campaigns. I sat with website owners and with artists who used crowdfunding to finance their projects and I let my fears surface in front of them. This is how I found that befriending your fears is an important process that helps us choose the platform that suits us best.

Much to my joy, I found out that I wasn't the only one who's afraid. Apparently there is a "fear package" that is fairly common to whoever is trying to raise funds this way. These fears derive mainly from the fact that the process is carried out with full transparency and displays the results in real time. In talking with Eliea Alon-Hacohen, the CEO of the platform I chose to use, I learned that it is also the system's strength. The transparency is reassuring for the supporters and helps them feel closer to the cause, resulting in a community that is formed and becomes the wind under the artist's wings.

OUT OF THIS INSIGHT I IMPLORE YOU: SILENCE THOSE FEARS AND PUT THEM TO REST. SEDATE THEM WITH COURAGE THAT IS BUILT OUT OF FAITH AND FOLLOW THAT FAITH UNTIL YOU REACH YOUR GOAL.

Human history is full of groundbreaking people who followed through with their truth. Just to name two very different ones: Galileo Galilei, who insisted that the world is revolving around its own axis and was persecuted by the Church for that. And Tom Hanks, who put his money and reputation on the line for a little movie that ended up being a huge blockbuster: *My Big Fat Greek Wedding.*

68 | INTERESTED IN CROWDFUNDING?
| COME ON THEN...

THE PLATFORM

You can find many Internet websites where you can set up a campaign page. I strongly recommend that you visit all of them, focusing on campaigns that fit the field of your interest or the most successful ones. Start exploring their success and failure rates, check the variety of rewards they offer their supporters, their conduct with the community, the quality of the communication and frequency of updates. Eventually you need to check: how do you feel about your experience on the campaign page? Would you have joined as a supporter? Try to isolate the reasons for your decision.

THE EMOTION BUTTON

Why should people support my idea?

That is the question that everybody who starts a crowdfunding campaign asks. Well, the answer is that people want to take a part in the success of an idea or a project. Crowdfunding creates the opportunity for supporters to have a direct communication line to the artist, who becomes available and approachable for them. That rationale is clearly manifested in this quote by Kevin Kelly, the founding executive editor of *Wired* magazine:

IT IS MY BELIEF THAT AUDIENCES WANT TO PAY CREATORS. FANS LIKE TO REWARD ARTISTS, MUSICIANS, AUTHORS AND THE LIKE WITH THE TOKENS OF THEIR APPRECIATION, BECAUSE IT ALLOWS THEM TO CONNECT. BUT THEY WILL ONLY PAY IF IT IS VERY EASY TO DO, A REASONABLE AMOUNT, AND THEY FEEL CERTAIN THE MONEY WILL DIRECTLY BENEFIT THE CREATORS.

When I researched the field of crowdfunding I encountered, among others, the project of an American biologist. He offered a product he called a "mini museum" (with samples of rocks, insects and other natural elements) and tried to raise $35,000 for developing this product. He raised a legendary amount of a million dollars within two months, which was far above his target budget. On the other hand, I encountered many projects that seemed promising (because of their interesting idea or the famous artist behind them), but failed miserably because they were not managed or communicated in a clear and compelling manner (Remember? Properly phrasing and focusing your dream before shouting and distributing it has an immense value).

ADDED VALUE

Do you want people to support your dream? Promise them an added value! It's important for your project to create value both for the supporter and for the community and society. If the aim of the project is just to better your own situation, there is great doubt as to whether you will succeed in raising your target budget. An explanation such as "I want to record a CD" or "I want to film a documentary about my grandfather" will not necessarily make people reach into their wallet.

Let's say you want to record your first CD. Express the depth of the materials and messages you want to convey in it, write the added value that your supporters will benefit from. Be involved in your community, document your work before and during the campaign, share, motivate. Your community will join this experience of value and will want to share the opportunity to promote and finance the project.

BOTTOM LINE

After you choose the website that you feel will fit your needs, send a personal email to the manager and ask to meet him/her. Make sure you identify with the website's values and find out how much they charge for commission at the end of the campaign (usually 10–15 percent). Ask about further fees that they may charge you at the end of the campaign.

YOUR COMMUNITY

Long before you start your campaign, build your community in social networks. Add friends to your different profiles, make comments on posts in other profiles, interact and "prepare the field" for action.

A fund-raising campaign is your campaign. It may at times feel a little bit like an election campaign, because along with the funds, you also receive a lot of sympathy and public attention. The website will update you about every new supporter and cause your mobile phone to keep beeping with new messages and comments. You are the owner of the campaign.

The campaign will also require a lot of your hard labor. Hours of answering emails, phone calls, explaining your project, recruiting people to your idea—both people you know and curious strangers who want to know how it all started. You will have to patiently explain to everybody what the project means for you and for them even if it's the eighth time over.

During the length of the campaign, aside from my Internet activity, I printed postcards with an explanation for how to find my project's web page and how to easily understand the different possibilities of supporting it. I carried those postcards on me for the duration of the project and presented one to everyone I met and encouraged them to join my community of supporters.

EXPRESSING YOUR DREAM WITH TRANSPARENCY

Express your dream well and remember—proper phrasing and publicity! Explain why you chose to raise the money this way and what value your project offers the world. Make sure you get your supporters excited about the project. Make sure you create real value for them, both content-wise and reward-wise, in return for the money that is entrusted to you.

More than once, I found myself financially supporting other people's dreams when I found their ideas moving. Publishing an Ethiopian cookbook, the proceeds of which were dedicated to empowering children of the Ethiopian community. A young man who had lost a lot of weight and needed funding for an operation to cut off his flabby skin.

THE REAL "LIKE"

The support of the crowd in your campaign—that is the real "like," not absentmindedly clicking "likes" on our friends' statuses. It is a process that comes from a real and deep involvement.

The first ones to support your project will be your close circles. Family, friends, and virtual friends. It's important to prepare the people around you for the upcoming campaign, so that they will be the first to recruit. They will later expose the project to their close circles and echo your messages that you have written on your campaign page or Facebook page, by sharing it or commenting on it. Having an initial substantial amount of money in the campaign's account will encourage others to join. Success is contagious. People want to take part in success.

You have the power to motivate people of different circles with a clear message, high value, and a wide variety of rewards.

A person from a distant circle who is exposed to your campaign will not rush to his wallet just yet. He will first weigh the significance of your project for him. Joining may take him a few days, or a few more exposures to your message.

Later, he will have to go fetch his wallet, take out his credit card, fill his details in the website, and approve the transaction. Even if he shared the project with his friends, or clicked "like" on it, there are still many opportunities for him to change his mind and decide not to give you his money. So what will make people eventually support your project out of all other ones? What will motivate them to open their wallet for you? Mostly the fact that you have succeeded in selling them value and emotion, and not just a project.

A CONTINUOUS, ENRICHING DIALOGUE

For the artist, the magic of the Internet crowdfunding campaign is the direct and un-mediated communication line to the community. Each supporter chose his preferred gift, agreed to share the project with his friends, and dedicated his money, time, and attention to the artist's success. This is a generosity that cannot be taken for granted. It has a great and significant value during the campaign and an enormous and continuous value after the campaign ends.

☑

During the sixty days of the campaign I published sixteen updates, which means that I communicated with my community every three days on average. My grateful communications were always accompanied by an invitation to derive more value from the project, whether by adding more rewards or an option to redeem some of the rewards before the campaign even ended. In addition, I opened a private Facebook group for the supporters who supported my projects with thousands of shekels, where I shared new developments and progress with the group, new connections, initiatives, and cooperation. I also used the group for brainstorming ideas for new rewards that might be exciting to the existing supporters, as well as the potential ones. This was how rewards like an intimate dinner at my house and partnership in proceeds from translating the book to five more languages were initiated.

When the campaign ended I started supplying the rewards. This gave me another means of communication that helped me reach all of the supporters in order to keep updating them about new developments in the project.

A few days before the end of the campaign, a close friend said she couldn't hear about *The List* anymore! She said I was nagging.

"That's right," I answered. "I'm nagging and when this is over in a few days, I will have over a quarter of a million shekels to realize my dream."

69 | OVERCOMING OTHER PEOPLE'S OBJECTIONS

SOMETIMES IN ORDER TO GET YOUR LIST TO WORK, THIS IS WHAT YOU WILL HAVE TO DO: BREAK DOWN OTHER PEOPLE'S OBJECTIONS.

Objections are a result of an untreated fear, or lack of faith. Your objectors are relatives of the toxic people, but if the toxic people at least listen to your dreams, the objectors will not even listen. They stifled their own dreams a long time ago and now they want to stifle yours.

Someone once left a sarcastic message on *The List* blog:

> Here is my list—world peace, global democracy, a social democrat Middle East, avenge the World Bank and the International Monetary Fund, eliminate hunger and eradicate poverty, cut the capitol's connections to capital, stop alienation and bring back community. Do you think that if 50 friends share it then it will happen, or does it only work in lists that set capitalist goals?

Since I always enjoy talking to my objectors, I asked her in return why she was being so cynical. Her reply was "You and I don't live in the same reality and don't speak the same language. When my dreams include an iPhone 5 or meeting Oprah Winfrey, we'll talk."

I don't know the girl who responded with such hostility, but I encountered quite a few objectors just like her in my lectures. They always find explanations and excuses for why my lists succeed and theirs don't. They explain to me that I'm famous, make a good living, and have a lot of friends on the Internet, on Facebook, and on my website. While that is true, I was not born in New York to a mega-rich father nor was I famous or well-connected until I started writing lists and developing my talents and connections in order to achieve self-fulfillment.

I also came across many who explained to me that writing lists is a privilege saved for well-fed people who are not weighed down by their mortgage and whose salary gets them safely to the end of the month. It's true that people who struggle with debt and daily survival have less emotional energy available to dream big dreams, and to them I would suggest writing an emergency list (just like the one I wrote when I was in a truly dire situation) that will help them improve the situation they are in. Many carry religious beliefs and faiths. I believe that our lives are in our hands.

I'VE SEEN MANY PEOPLE IN MY LIFE WHO HAVE PROVEN THIS CLAIM. PEOPLE WHO HAD GOTTEN INTO BIG PERSONAL AND FINANCIAL PROBLEMS AND OVERCAME THEM WITH A CONSCIOUS DECISION TO GET OUT OF THE RUT, SHARE THEIR PROBLEMS, AND ASK FOR HELP IN ORDER TO OVERCOME EVERY OBSTACLE.

A few weeks before printing the first edition of this book I was interviewed on TV about *The List*. The makeup artist recognized me and asked if I thought anyone could realize their dream. I answered that I really think so, and that it all depends on gaining experience in doing it.

"I had my makeup done so many times in TV studios," I said, giving her an example from her own field, "that I could take your sponges now and do your makeup. It wouldn't be perfect, but it wouldn't be bad. I've learned something from watching makeup artists. If I thought that my future lay in the makeup profession, I would have gone to study it and became a professional makeup artist."

IF WE REALLY WANT TO, WE WILL LEARN HOW TO REALIZE OUR DREAMS.

70 | IS EVERY LIST
VALUABLE?

Absolutely! Every list is as valuable as gold for the person who wrote it. Even if it seems like your list consists of items that are not so important or impressive, it is still your key to change.

A list of dreams doesn't have to be grandiose. Even if it doesn't consist of items regarding the straightening the Tower of Pisa, or the welfare of cattle herds around the world, it is still our own and is there to help us realize our own private dreams.

A dream can be small and modest, but once it is realized, it makes our lives better and more satisfying.

AND WHAT IF EVERYBODY WROTE LISTS?

When I was still writing this book I spent a few days in Berlin for work. I met with an Israeli friend who lives there and told him about *The List* project.

My friend, who wasn't familiar with the project, listened carefully and then said, "It sounds very interesting and important. But you know what the problem is with such a book? That millions of people will start writing lists and shouting them out loud."

I couldn't see where the problem was.

"The problem is that not everybody can realize their dreams," he continued. "The planet is too crowded for that, there isn't enough space for everybody. Just imagine if everybody wrote the item 'publish a book.' There aren't enough bookstores in the world for that!"

I smiled.

My friend's fears don't make sense to me. After all, there is always more room in the world for more good things. My journeys with *The List* and with self-fulfillment don't oblige me to check off each and every item. A part of the system is re-examining whether we can do things and whether we still possess the will and enthusiasm to dissolve the difficulties as we come across them.

True, there are people whose efforts to realize their dream exhaust them and so they eventually let it go. The ability to let go is also a sort of an achievement in my opinion. From the moment you decide to let go of a dream, you also let go of the frustration of not having tried, or missing out on it. An unrealized dream can turn into a nightmare.

Someone I know has a long standing dream of learning to sculpt.

"What's stopping you? Go register for a sculpting course already!" I tried to prod her.

"I'm afraid I'll find out I'm really bad at it," she replied.

"So you prefer to live with an unrealized dream? Aren't you better off registering? Worst-case scenario is that you find out you don't even have the basic ability and then you can give up that dream and clear the space in your head and heart for a new one!"

Instead of answering me, she quickly phoned a studio that had been recommended to her. And it turned out she was a pretty good sculptress!

This was my reply to my friend in Berlin:

"WE LIVE IN TIMES OF REALITY TV SHOWS THAT TEACH US THAT IN LIFE THERE IS ONE WINNER AND MANY LOSERS, WHILE REALITY ITSELF IS VERY DIFFERENT. IN LIFE THERE ARE MANY WINNERS WHO REACH FIRST PLACE, AND MANY MORE WHO REACH SECOND PLACE."

My friend seemed pensive. He gazed at his beer and then replied, "Listen, you have a system! But it's your system and it's right and effective for you, but not necessarily for others."

This is also a sentence I know all too well. It's clear to me that *The List* is working for me, and that the trigger for my first list was the accident I had when I was sixteen. On the other hand, thousands of people around the world have written lists (some more accurate than others) and shared them on the blog. *The List* helped them all to better their lives. They moved to better jobs, found love, adopted a baby, earned money, ticked off routine tasks, met their teenage idol, or went on a trip they have been dreaming about their whole life.

71 | DO NOT LET THE IDEAS RUN AWAY

There is nothing I detest more than the waste of a good idea. Waiting for "the right moment" means letting others beat you to the punch. They don't say that great minds think alike for nothing. You have a brilliant idea? It is most likely to pop up in someone else's mind somewhere around the world. Do you want to forfeit your dreams?

THE STORY OF *THE LIST* IS, INDEED, MY STORY. THE ACCIDENT THAT HAPPENED TO ME AT AGE SIXTEEN WAS THE DEFINING MOMENT OF MY LIFE. DON'T WAIT FOR SUCH A MOMENT TO ROCK YOUR LIFE AND REMIND YOU THAT YOUR TOMORROWS ARE NUMBERED. AN EFFECTIVE LIST HAS THE POWER TO CHANGE A LIFE AND THE CROWD HAS THE ENERGY OF A NUCLEAR REACTOR.

WRITE
YOUR LISTS.
NOW.

72 | MY NEW LIST

In order for us to be able to keep in touch after you finish reading this book, I decided to share my new list with you.

Yes, I already have a new list and it is composed of, how surprising, ten items I intend to realize in the next 400 days.

I will start a new journey to fulfillment as soon as the book you are holding is published.

The documentation of my new journey will be found in *The List* website in the address: www.uv-tlv.com (write "The List" in the search tab). You are more than welcome to try and help me realize my new dreams. I love getting help.

Here are the items of my new list:

- ☐ Spread the message of *The List* in a few languages and give lectures in Israel and around the world
- ☐ Get *The List* to Oprah Winfrey, offer her a professional collaboration (some dreams are carried from one list to the other until they come true!) and, of course, interview her
- ☐ Recruit staff that will help me establish the "Shekel a Day" foundation that will provide happy life experiences for children in need
- ☐ Learn to cook
- ☐ Despite my work load, household chores, and parental duties— make sure to have dinner with friends at least once a week (refresh and enlarge my list of friends)
- ☐ Make time in my schedule to fly to Australia for a two-week trip minimum (I already have a place to stay and the air fare)
- ☐ Develop my talk show format, *Private Screening*, until I find a production house for it
- ☐ Write a theatre play
- ☐ Produce a one act play in which I will also act
- ☐ Make sure I take one day a week off work, away from the computer

☑

If you've come this far, I assume that you've already taken in my message about dreams: focus on them, publish them, and spread them out to the world.

Here is another little dream I had. I wanted this book to reach as many people as possible, all over the world. The power to help me is in your hands! If you identify with my ideas, I would be happy if you can spread the message and "shout out" the existence of the book.

TAKE A PICTURE OF YOURSELF HOLDING THE BOOK, UPLOAD YOUR LISTS ONTO THE INTERNET, QUOTE PARTS OF IT AND POST THEM ON YOUR FACEBOOK WALL, OR ON ANY OTHER SOCIAL NETWORK. THAT WAY YOU CAN HELP THE LIST REACH AS MANY PEOPLE AS POSSIBLE, AND TOGETHER WE CAN CREATE AN INTERNATIONAL COMMUNITY SHARING A COMMON LANGUAGE.

If you want to comment, ask questions, make suggestions, argue with me, support me, or tell me about anything in the book, you can find me here:

Email: uvtlv1@gmail.com

Facebook: yuval abramovitz

Twitter: uvtlv

Instagram: uv

My website: http://uv-tlv.com/en/

The List Facebook page: The List—Shout Out Your Dreams

To book a lecture (in English): adi.thelist@gmail.com

ACKNOWLEDGMENTS

✓ First and foremost, I'm grateful to the thousands of people around the world who have shown interest in *The List* project from the moment it went on the air. I want to thank all of those who expressed their willingness to help without expecting anything in return, and who opened their homes and their hearts without hesitation. I would also like to thank thousands of people who commented, replied, listed, promoted others' lists, and sent me theirs, and to all those who provided constructive criticism, thus helping me to focus my idea.

✓ Thanks to Tamara Moyal, the most talented graphic designer I've had the pleasure of working with! Your mind is flowing with creativity.

✓ Thanks to Anat Lev Adler, a close friend and a perceptive editor, for counseling and upgrading the book throughout the writing process.

✓ Thanks to Tali Asraf Juran, for the meticulous translation, for investing yourself in the work, and for succeeding in breathing my Israeli breath and so accurately translating it to English.

✓ To Julie Phelps, for both the British and American eyes that looked at the book and tightened it even more.

✓ Thanks to all the promoters of the funding campaign, who preordered the book and bought lecture tickets and other gifts, financially supporting the project. This book would not exist without you. Not even thousands of thanks are enough to express my honest gratitude to each and every one of you.

✓ A big special thank you to Ari Koka, Jonni zicholtz, Eran Talmor, Leah Yaffe-Talmor, Betty and Eitan Yaffe, Bracha Lite, Lior Talmor, Golan Bar-Or, Efrat Enzel, Adi Arklis, Golan Leinman, Ronit Yurslavitz, Ira Markovitz Twig, Lilach Vidal, Arlet Bill, Dor DiMarimsky, Noa Bodner, Tali Asraf Juran, Ido Juran and Orit Gill, for being brave enough to invest large amounts of money in *The List* project and expressing your absolute trust in me and the idea.

✓ To Benny, Tali and Nave Karmi, for your hard work promoting the book on Amazon and the support along the way.

✓ To my new friends at Skyhorse Publishing. Thank you so much for your trust in me and mainly for the great pleasure of working with you.

THANK ALL OF YOU WHO HAVE BOTHERED TO COME THIS FAR AND READ THIS PAGE.